10,001

Quotes & Sayings

World's Largest Collection
of Quotes and Sayings

Volume I

SUSHEEL LADWA

Mamata and Vishwanath Ladwa

My Mother and Father

"All I Am, I Owe To You"

ACKNOWLEDGMENTS

Writing a book starts as a hobby, becomes a passion, and rules your dreams until it becomes a reality. I gave it time because it is my passion. I want to acknowledge the people that gave their time and support to help realize my passion.

I wanted to thank my wife, Preetha, for her patience, love and support through the blur of day and night with a month old baby. This book would not have been possible without her. Every time there is a knock on my office door, there enters a big beautiful smile that makes it all worth it – Ruhi, my daughter, my friend, my little philosopher and guide. The new bundle of joy of the family – Syon, he is a month old but has shown who the boss is.

My brother, Sunil, my sister-in-law, Sumitra, and kids, Shreya, Kushi, and Arya, for their love and faith in me.

Last but not the least, my editor Jeffery Watson, for all the cattle he chased while editing my book – Thank you!

.

PREFACE

The only reason history repeats itself is because the human race does not learn. Think about the history of mankind and all the combined experiential knowledge through the ages available for us to learn from – it could make our lives simpler, fuller and happier.

When I read the oldest books known to mankind, I found something very striking - they are all written in verses that are not more than a few sentences. That was the "ah ha" moment for me, our brains are best at capturing and understanding life's concepts in short power packed sentences. This revelation led me to start collecting quotes and sayings.

I believe the best way to pass on the wealth of knowledge of mankind is to collect pearls of wisdom uttered as quotes and sayings. This book is an attempt to create the largest collection of quotes and sayings. The book presents quotes and sayings randomly to keep the "surprise" of life alive.

When Mahatma Gandhi, personification of truth, nonviolence, equality, and peace received a hateful letter, he read the letter with a smile and saved the paper clip. Someone asked him why he saved the paper clip and trashed the letter. His answer, "The paper clip was the only useful thing I found in the letter." This book is a collection of those paper clips, that will trigger a thought, change an action, set the tone for the day or just make you smile.

QUOTES

&

SAYINGS

Change before you have to. - Jack Welch

Genius is one percent inspiration and ninety-nine percent perspiration. - Thomas Edison

---

The only way to do great work is to love what you do. If you haven't found it yet, keep looking. Don't settle. - Steve Jobs

---

When all you own is a hammer, every problem starts looking like a nail. - Abraham Maslow

---

Success is walking from failure to failure with no loss of enthusiasm. - Winston Churchill

---

We are living in a world, where what we earn is a function of what we learn. - Bill Clinton

Someone's sitting in the shade today because someone planted a tree a long time ago. - Warren Buffett

Sometimes the road less traveled is less traveled for a reason. - Jerry Seinfeld

Give me a place to stand, and I shall move the world. - Archimedes

You can do a lot with diplomacy, but with diplomacy backed up by force you can get a lot more done. - Kofi Annan

An eye for an eye, and soon the whole world is blind.
- Mahatma Gandhi

Speak softly and carry a big stick. - Theodore
Roosevelt

If you think you can do a thing or think you can't do
a thing, you're right. - Henry Ford

"Mind is never a problem, mindset is" - Narendra
Modi, Indian PM Aspirant

Only those most adaptive to change will survive. –
Charles Darwin

Failure is not an option. - Gene Kranz, Apollo 13

Am I not destroying my enemies when I make friends of them? - Abraham Lincoln

---

A crisis is a terrible thing to waste. - Dick Clark, CEO Merck

---

If I had asked my customers what they wanted, they'd have said a faster horse. - Henry Ford

---

Everyone rises to their level of incompetence. - Laurence J. Peter

---

If you want to live a happy life, tie it to a goal, not to people or objects. - Albert Einstein

Strategy without tactics is the slowest route to victory. Tactics without strategy is the noise before defeat. - Sun Tzu

Reading maketh a full man, conference a ready man, writing an exact man.

You can have everything in life that you want if you just give enough other people what they want. - Zig Ziglar

Perpetual optimism is a force multiplier. - Colin Powell

The best way to keep one's word is not to give it. - Napoleon Bonaparte

---

The man who does not work for the love of work but only for money is not likely to neither make money nor find much fun in life. - Charles M. Schwab

---

If each of us would only sweep their own doorstep, the whole world would be clean - Mother Teresa

---

I detest racialism, because I regard it as a barbaric thing, whether it comes from a black man or a white man. - Nelson Mandela

---

There are in fact two things, science and opinion; the former begets knowledge, the latter ignorance. - Hippocrates

If A is a success in life, then A equals x plus y plus z. Work is x; y is play; and z is keeping your mouth shut. - Albert Einstein

The past is a ghost, the future a dream, and all we ever have is now. - Bill Cosby

Do what you can, with what you have, where you are - Theodore Roosevelt

I am prepared to die, but there is no cause for which I am prepared to kill. - Mahatma Gandhi

It's not the size of the dog in the fight; it's the size of the fight in the dog. - Mark Twain

To hell with circumstances. I create opportunities. - Bruce Lee

---

The laws of gravity cannot be held responsible for people falling in love. - Albert Einstein

---

You can get much further with a kind word and a gun than you can with a kind word alone. - Al Capone

---

To be successful, you have to have your heart in your business, and your business in your heart - Thomas Watson, Sr.

Share your knowledge. It's a way to achieve immortality. - Dalai Lama

Holding on to anger is like grasping a hot coal with the intent of throwing it at someone else; you are the one who gets burned. - Siddhartha Buddha

You can't build a reputation on what you are going to do. - Henry Ford

The greatest discovery of all time is that a person can change his future by merely changing his attitude. - Oprah Winfrey

First think, second believe, third dream and finally dare - Walt Disney

You put water into a cup, it becomes the cup. You put water into a teapot, it becomes the teapot. Now water can crash, drip, flow...be water my friend. - Bruce Lee

Success is a lousy teacher. It seduces smart people into thinking they can't lose. - Bill Gates

Success does not consist in never making mistakes but in never making the same one a second time. - George Bernard Shaw

The invisible hand of the market always moves faster and better than the heavy hand of government. - Mitt Romney

Government's view of the economy could be summed up in a few short phrases: If it moves, tax it. If it keeps moving, regulate it. And if it stops moving, subsidize it. - Ronald Reagan

I will tell you how to become rich. Close the doors. Be fearful when others are greedy. Be greedy when others are fearful. - Warren Buffet

Success, the real success, does not depend upon the position you hold but upon how you carry yourself in that position. - Theodore Roosevelt

If you are going through hell, keep going. - Winston Churchill

The fight is won or lost far away from the witnesses, behind the lines, in the gym, and out there on the road; long before I dance under those lights. - Muhammad Ali

I want to put a ding in the universe. - Steve Jobs

Courage is what it takes to stand up and speak.
Courage is also what it takes to sit down and listen. -
Winston Churchill

Most of the important things in the world have been
accomplished by people who have kept on trying
when there seemed to be no hope at all. - Dale
Carnegie

You must be the change you wish to see in the world.
– Gandhi

Faith is taking the first step even when you don't see
the whole staircase. - Martin Luther King Jr.

People are about as happy as they make up their
minds to be. - Abraham Lincoln

We always overestimate the change that will occur in the next two years and underestimate the change that will occur in the next ten. - Bill Gates

You only have to do a very few things right in your life so long as you don't do too many things wrong. - Warren Buffett

Nonviolence is the greatest force at the disposal of mankind. It is mightier than the mightiest weapon of destruction devised by the ingenuity of man. - Mahatma Gandhi

If I have ever made any valuable discoveries, it has been owing more to patient attention than to any other talent. – Isaac Newton

Make everything as simple as possible, but not simpler. - Albert Einstein

I have not failed. I've just found 10,000 ways that won't work. - Thomas Edison

If you judge people, you have no time to love them. - Mother Teresa

Just as a solid rock is not shaken by the storm, even so the wise are not affected by praise or blame. - Gautama Buddha in the Dhammapada

I'm for truth, no matter who tells it. I'm for justice, no matter who it's for or against. - Malcolm X

The test of our progress is not whether we add more to the abundance of those who have much; it is whether we provide enough for those who have too little. - Franklin D. Roosevelt

---

Dignity does not consist in possessing honors, but in deserving them. - Aristotle

---

Life is what happens to you while you're busy making other plans. - John Lennon

---

Hatred does not cease by hatred at any time; hatred ceases by love.

It ought to be remembered that there is nothing more difficult to take in hand, more perilous to conduct, or more uncertain in its success, than to take the lead in the introduction of a new order of things. - Niccol Machiavelli

This chance won't come around again. - Michelle Obama

True originality consists not in a new manner but in a new vision. - Edith Wharton

Love is life. All, everything that I understand, I understand only because I love. - Leo Tolstoy

I will either find a way, or make one. - Hannibal

It's always worthwhile to make others aware of their worth. - Malcolm Forbes

---

The first of April is the day we remember what we are the other 364 days of the year. - Mark Twain

---

Do not that to another, which thou wouldest not have done to thy selfe. - Thomas Hobbes

---

The length of one's days matters less than the love of one's family and friends. - Gerald Ford

---

It is better that ten guilty persons escape, than that one innocent suffer. - William Blackstone

---

You can only be young once but you can be immature forever. - Dave Barry

I remain just one thing, and one thing only - and that is a clown. It places me on a far higher plane than any politician. - Charlie Chaplin

You climb to reach the summit, but once there, discover that all roads lead down. - Stanisław Lem

The future belongs to those who believe in the beauty of their dreams. - Eleanor Roosevelt

Men make their own history, but they do not make it just as they please; they do not make it under circumstances chosen by themselves, but under circumstances directly encountered, given and transmitted from the past. - Karl Marx

If you go looking for a friend, you're going to find they're very scarce. If you go out to be a friend, you'll find them everywhere. - Zig Ziglar

Evil spreads with the wind; truth is capable of spreading even against it. - Paramahansa Yogananda

Man is free at the instant he wants to be. - Voltaire

If I had to choose, I would rather have birds than airplanes. - Charles Lindbergh

You cannot force ideas. Successful ideas are the result of slow growth. Ideas do not reach perfection in a day, no matter how much study is put upon them. - Alexander Graham Bell

That best portion of a good man's life, - His little, nameless, unremembered acts of kindness and of love. - William Wordsworth

When the sword is once drawn, the passions of men observe no bounds of moderation. - Alexander Hamilton

Unless you choose to do great things with it, it makes no difference how much you are rewarded, or how much power you have. - Oprah Winfrey

Our destiny is frequently met in the very paths we take to avoid it. - Jean de La Fontaine

All I am I owe to my mother. I attribute all my success in life to the moral, intellectual and physical education I received from her. - George Washington

The person who will bear much shall have much to bear, all the world through. - Samuel Richardson

The ambition of the greatest men of our generation has been to wipe every tear from every eye. That may be beyond us, but so long as there are tears and suffering, so long our work will not be over. - Jawaharlal Nehru

For the first time ever, blogs convert readers and viewers into writers. And YouTube turns them into directors. - Seth Godin, Meatball Sundae

Someone, somewhere has to have a better answer. - Jack Welch

(Reality) is that which, when you stop believing in it, doesn't go away. - Philip K. Dick

We do no great things. We do only small things with great love. - Mother Teresa

———————— ~ ————————

Once you wake up thought in a man you can never put it to sleep again. - Zora Neale Hurston

———————— ~ ————————

Good artists copy, great artists steal. - Picasso

———————— ~ ————————

Reality's a nice place to visit, but you wouldn't want to live there. - John Barth

———————— ~ ————————

Numbers aren't bad by themselves, but maybe what we're counting is. - Dave Gibbons

———————— ~ ————————

The fact is, you're always on the record, everyone is a critic (or could be), and the Web remembers forever. - Seth Godin, Meatball Sundae

---

The average man, who does not know what to do with this life, wants another one which shall last forever. - Anatole Francois Thibault

---

A woman's guess is much more accurate than a man's certainty. - Kipling

---

Never try to be an expert if you are not. Build on your strengths and find strong people to do the other necessary tasks. - Peter Drucker

---

It's impossible to stand out when your goal in life is to fit in.

You miss 100% of the shots you never take. - Wayne Gretzky (the Great One)

———————～———————

Privacy is dead. Get over it. - Scott McNealy, Sun Microsystems founder

———————～———————

Figure out who you are and then do it on purpose. - Dolly Parton

———————～———————

At the moment of commitment, the universe conspires to assist you. - Goethe

———————～———————

When you think you have all the answers, you don't even ask the questions. - Peter Drucker

———————～———————

It's Google's world. We just live in it. - Chris Tulles, vice-president, Topix Inc.

———————～——————

The secret of success in war is learning what lies on the other side of the hill. - Duke of Wellington

———————～——————

The trouble with most of us is that we would rather be ruined by praise than saved by criticism. - Norman Vincent Peale

———————～——————

It is the enemy who can truly teach us to practice the virtues of compassion and tolerance. - 14th Dalai Lama

———————～——————

Ambition is so powerful a passion in the human breast, that however high we reach we are never satisfied. - Niccoló Machiavelli

A business has to be involving, it has to be fun, and it has to exercise your creative instincts. - Richard Branson

---

Where ignorance is our master, there is no possibility of real peace. - Dalai Lama

---

The majority of men meet with failure because of their lack of persistence in creating new plans to take the place of those which fail. - Napoleon Hill

---

Don't confuse having a career with having a life. - Hillary Clinton

---

An ounce of loyalty is worth a pound of cleverness. - Elbert Hubbard

You can have it all. You just can't have it all at once. - Oprah Winfrey

---

It is easy enough to be friendly to one's friends. But to befriend the one who regards himself as your enemy is the quintessence of true religion. - Mahatma Gandhi

---

There are only two ways to live your life. One is as though nothing is a miracle. The other is as though everything is a miracle. - Albert Einstein

---

There are few things as useless - if not as dangerous - as the right answer to the wrong question. - Peter Drucker

---

Silence is one great art of conversation. - William Hazlitt

Man is born free; and everywhere he is in chains. - Jean-Jacques Rousseau

To handle yourself, use your head. To handle others, use your heart. - Eleanor Roosevelt

To keep your marriage brimming, with love in the living cup, whenever you're wrong admit it, whenever you're right, shut up. - Ogden Nash

Without the ceaseless work ethic, Michael Jordan is merely another talented athlete gliding through an admirable career, but nothing historic.

If you love someone, set them free. If they come back they are yours; if they don't, they never were. - Buddhist Proverb

Aim at Heaven and you will get Earth thrown in. Aim at Earth and you get neither. - C.S. Lewis

---

Execution is the strategy. - Sam Geist

He, who can properly summarize many ideas in a brief statement, is a wise man. - Euripides

---

No organization will rise above the passion of the leader. - Ken Blanchard

---

If you had to identify, in one word, the reason why the human race has not achieved, and never will achieve its full potential, that word would be meetings. - Dave Barry

---

The only good ideas are the ones I can take credit for. - R. Stevens

If you are not failing every now and again, it's a sign you're playing it safe. - Woody Allen

The man who knows how will always have a job. The man who knows why will always be his boss. - Ralph Waldo Emerson

We have always been shameless about stealing great ideas. - Steve Jobs

Questioning yourself must become a habit, one strong enough to surmount the obstacles of overconfidence and dejection. - Gary Kasparov

Creativity is just connecting things. - Steve Jobs

If forty million people say a foolish thing it does not become a wise one, but the wise man is foolish to give them the lie. - W. Somerset Maugham

It's not enough not to be evil. We also actively try to be good. - Sergey Brin, Google

The leader finds greatness in the group. - Theodore Roosevelt

Do you want to sell sugar water for the rest of your life, or do you want to change the world? - Steve Jobs challenging John Sculley to leave Pepsi and come work for Apple

We learn from experience that men never learn from experience. - George Bernard Shaw

Words are words, explanations are explanations, promises are promises - but only performance is reality. - Harold Geneen, CEO of ITT

People who enjoy meetings should not be in charge of anything. - Thomas Sowell

Orville Wright did not have a pilot's license. - Gordon MacKenzie, Orbiting the Giant

Example is the most potent of all things . . . You must feel that the most effective way in which you can preach is by your practice. - Theodore Roosevelt

Not all readers are leaders but all leaders must be readers. - Harry Truman

Life is the sum of all your choices. - Camus

I hear and I forget. I see and I remember. I do and I understand. - Confucius

When you discover you are riding a dead horse. Dismount. - Dakota Indian proverb

I refuse to join any club that would have me as a member. - Mark Twain

I was surprised to find myself so much fuller of faults than I had imagined. - Ben Franklin

---

The first and best victory is to conquer self. - Plato

Your lack of prior planning does not constitute an emergency on my part.

In war, resolution; in defeat, defiance; in victory, magnanimity; in peace, good will. - Churchill

---

As soon as any man has ceased to be able to learn, his usefulness as a teacher is at an end. When he himself can't learn, he has reached the stage where other people can learn from him. - Theodore Roosevelt

---

Laughter is the shortest distance between two people.
- Victor Borge

Ｉ

A friend in power is a friend lost. - Henry Brooks
Adams

Ｉ

A well-spent day brings happy sleep. - Leonardo da
Vinci

Ｉ

Judge your success by what you had to give up to get
it. - 14th Dalai Lama

Ｉ

You are never too old to set another goal or to dream
a new dream. - C.S. Lewis

Ｉ

The first responsibility of a leader is to define reality. The last is to say thank you. In between, the leader is a servant. - Max de Pree

Always try to be a little kinder than is necessary. - James Barrie

Next to acquiring good friends, the best acquisition is that of good books. - Colton

"I do not believe you can do today's job with yesterday's methods and be in business tomorrow." - Nelson Jackson

"Do not say anything harsh, what you have said will be said back to you."

"Take time to be quiet, it is the opportunity to see yourself."

"Experience is a hard teacher because it gives the test first, and the lesson afterwards."

"Have a heart that never hardens, a temper that never tires and a touch that never hurts."

"There are three ingredients in good life- learning, earning and enjoying what you do."

"If we think happy thoughts, we will be happy. If we think miserable thoughts, we will be miserable."

"Even if you are not responsible for your situation, you are responsible for your reaction to it."

When you were born, you cried and the world rejoiced. Live your life so that when you die, the world cries and you rejoice.

A small bit of tolerance expressed daily will reward you with peace, friendship and spiritual growth.

Learn to listen, and then listen to learn.

Arise! Awake! Stop not till the goal is reached. - Swami Vivekananda

Lose an hour in the morning and you will be looking for it the rest of the day! - Lord Chesterfield

―――――――∽―――――――

Today, give a stranger one of your smiles. It might be the only sunshine he sees all day.

―――――――∽―――――――

When it is the question of money, everybody is of the same religion.

―――――――∽―――――――

A statesman is one who desires to do something for his country, whereas a politician desires his country to do something for him. - Sir Malcom Hailey

―――――――∽―――――――

Do not pretend– be. Do not promise– act. Do not dream– realize.

―――――――∽―――――――

When I refuse to forgive, I am burning a bridge that someday I will need to pass over.

An optimist sees an opportunity in each calamity; a pessimist sees a calamity in every opportunity.

History repeats because man never learns.

Do not speak without thinking, do not act without reflecting. - Swami Sivananda

Brevity is the soul of wit.

A good woman is known by what she does, a good man by what he does not. - Helen Rowland

A man travels the world over in search of what he needs and returns home to find it. - George Moore

---

Defeat is not when you fall down; it is when you refuse to get up.

You can meet friends everywhere but you cannot meet enemies everywhere- you have to make them.

If two men agree on everything, you may be sure that one of them is doing all the thinking.

A little more determination, a little more pluck, a little more work that is luck.

The liar's punishment is not in the least that he is not believed, but that he cannot believe anyone else.

There are two ways of spreading light, to be the candle or the mirror that reflects it.

A wise man reflects before he speaks; a fool speaks and then reflects on what he has spoken.

No man is rich whose expenses exceed his means and no man is poor whose income exceeds his expenses.

Have confidence that if you have done a little thing well, you can do a bigger thing well too.

A guilty conscience needs no accuser

At the first cup a man drinks wine, at the second cup wine drinks wine, the third cup wine drinks the man.

A good leader takes a little more than his share of the blame, a little less than his share of the credit.

Speak not except what may benefit others or yourself. Avoid unimportant conversations.

It will be found an unjust and unwise jealousy to deprive a man of his natural liberty upon the supposition he may abuse it. - George Washington

The harder the conflict, the more glorious the triumph. What we obtain too cheap, we esteem too lightly. It is dearness only that gives everything its value. - Thomas Paine

The liberties of a people never were, nor ever will be, secure, when the transactions of their rulers may be concealed from them. - Patrick Henry

The United States stands at the pinnacle of world power. This is a solemn moment for the American democracy. For with primacy in power is joined an awe-inspiring accountability for the future. - Winston Churchill

You find out more about God from the Moral Law than from the universe in general, just as you find out more about a man by listening to his conversation than by looking at a house he has built. - C.S. Lewis

A single hour spent with a good book and a cup of tea can provide an entire day's worth of contentment

If eighty percent of your sales come from twenty percent of all of your items, just carry that twenty percent. - Henry Kissinger

Alas, I am dying beyond my means. - Oscar Wilde

When I'm writing, I know I'm doing the thing I was born to do. - Anne Sexton

I believe this government cannot endure permanently half slave and half free. - Abraham Lincoln

In Christianity, neither morality nor religion comes into contact with reality at any point. - Friedrich Nietzsche

People want to know why I do this, why I write such gross stuff. I like to tell them that I have the heart of a small boy... and I keep it in a jar on my desk. - Stephen King

Courage is the first of human qualities because it is the quality which guarantees all others. - Winston Churchill

You can bear your own faults, and why not a fault in your wife? - Benjamin Franklin

Glory is fleeting, but obscurity is forever. - Napoleon Bonaparte

There is no charm equal to tenderness of heart. - Jane Austen

---

Uncleanliness of the mind is far more dangerous than that of the body. The latter, however is an indication of the former.

The way to get started is to quit talking and begin doing. - Walt Disney

---

Brevity is the soul of lingerie. - Dorothy Parker

Nurture great thoughts, for you will never be higher than your thoughts. - Benjamin Disraeli

---

The degree of one's emotions varies inversely with one's knowledge of the facts: the less you know the hotter you get. - Bertrand Russell

———————～———————

Blood is the ink of our life's story. - Jason Mechalek

———————～———————

It is a man's own mind, not his enemy or foe, which lures him to evil ways. - Siddhartha Buddha

———————～———————

Drive your business. Let not your business drive you. - Benjamin Franklin

———————～———————

Mother and Mother Country are greater than heaven

———————～———————

The road to success and the road to failure are almost exactly the same. - Colin R. Davis

The dream is the small hidden door in the deepest and most intimate sanctum of the soul, which opens to that primeval cosmic night that was the soul long before there was conscious ego and will be the soul far beyond what a conscious ego could ever reach. - Carl Jung

One can resist the invasion of an army but one cannot resist the invasion of ideas. - Victor Hugo

Ten people who speak make more noise than ten thousand who are silent. - Napoleon Bonaparte

To win without risk is to triumph without glory. - Pierre Corneille

The winner is always part of the answer; the loser is always part of the problem

I shall not waste my days in trying to prolong them. - Ian Fleming

Forgiveness is not an occasional act: it is a permanent attitude. - Martin Luther King Jr.

I hate rap music, which to me sounds like a bunch of angry men shouting, possibly because the person who was supposed to provide them with a melody never showed up. - Dave Barry

Take what you require for your legitimate needs, and use the remainder for society. - Mahatma Gandhi

The man who carries a cat by the tail learns
something that can be learned in no other way. -
Mark Twain

———————～——————

Nobody has ever before asked the nuclear family to
live all by itself in a box the way we do. With no
relatives, no support, we've put it in an impossible
situation. - Margaret Mead

———————～——————

One's mind has a way of making itself up in the
background, and it suddenly becomes clear what one
means to do. - A. C. Benson

———————～——————

Liberty means responsibility. That is why most men
dread it. - George Bernard Shaw

———————～——————

Be good, see good, do good, and good will happen to
you.

Divide and rule, a sound motto. Unite and lead, a better one. - Johann Wolfgang von Goethe

He that is of opinion money will do everything, may well be suspected of doing anything for money.

We must sail sometimes with the wind and sometimes against it, but sail we must and not drift nor lie at anchor. - Oliver Wendell Holmes

Not education, but character is man's greatest need and man's greatest safeguard. - Spencer

There is no such thing as a good war and there is no such thing as a bad peace. - Benjamin Franklin

If you were to open up a baby's head- and I am not for a moment suggesting that you should- you would find nothing but an enormous drool gland. - Dave Barry

The only way to keep your health is to eat what you don't want, drink what you don't like, and do what you'd rather not. - Mark Twain

In business, I've discovered that my purpose is to do my best to my utmost ability every day. That's my standard. I learned early in my life that I had high standards. - Donald Trump

No one can earn a million dollars honestly. - William Jennings Bryan

A facility for quotation covers the absence of original thought. - Peter Wimsey

Wal-Mart, what's that? Do they, like, make walls there? - Paris Hilton

---

A yawn is a silent shout. - GK Chesterton

The great thing about democracy is that it gives every voter a chance to do something stupid. - Art Spander

---

The moment we want to believe something, we suddenly see all the arguments for it, and become blind to the arguments against it. - George Bernard Shaw

---

A very quiet and tasteful way to be famous is to have a famous relation. Then you cannot only be nothing, you can do nothing, too. - P.J. O'Rourke

The practice of art isn't to make a living. It's to make your soul grow. - Kurt Vonnegut

Wisdom stands at the turn in the road and calls upon us publicly, but we consider it false and despise its adherents. - Kahlil Gibran

Through pride we are ever deceiving ourselves. But deep down below the surface of the average conscience a still, small voice says to us, something is out of tune. - Carl Jung

Life does not teach us to expect nothing, but not to expect success to be the inevitable result of all our endeavors.

We become what we think about all day long. The question is, 'What do you think about?' - Wayne Dyer

There is no place to which we could flee from God which is outside God.

———————— ~~~ ————————

Forgive others often, yourself never. – Syrus

———————— ~~~ ————————

Money isn't the most important thing in life, but it's reasonably close to oxygen on the gotta have it scale. - Zig Ziglar

———————— ~~~ ————————

What we actually learn, from any given set of circumstances, determines whether we become increasingly powerless or more powerful. - Blaine Lee

———————— ~~~ ————————

The great virtue in life is real courage that knows how to face facts and live beyond them. - D.H. Lawrence

Like pride, greed is a great obstacle to advancement, and both of these must be mercilessly washed away. - Edward Bach

---

The beginnings of all things are small. – Cicero

Real loss is only possible when you love something more than you love yourself. - Robin Williams

---

Women love us for our defects. If we have enough of them, they will forgive us everything, even our gigantic intellects. - Oscar Wilde

---

Good friends, good books and a sleepy conscience: this is the ideal life. - Mark Twain

---

Every improvement in communication makes the bore more terrible. - Frank Moore Colby

———————～———————

You must not think me necessarily foolish because I am facetious, nor will I consider you necessarily wise because you are grave. - Sydney Smith

———————～———————

Men can be analyzed, women merely adored. - Oscar Wilde

———————～———————

Experts often possess more data than judgment. - Colin Powell

———————～———————

I love mankind; its people I can't stand. - Charles Schulz

———————～———————

A poor but humble man who gives nothing to charity is preferable to a rich but haughty man who does. - Nachman of Bratslav

A man is but the product of his thoughts. What he thinks, he becomes. - Mahatma Gandhi

I think and think for months and years, ninety-nine times, the conclusion is false. The hundredth time I am right. - Albert Einstein

Most of the problems a President has to face have their roots in the past. - Harry Truman

If destruction be our lot, we must ourselves be its author and finisher. As a nation of freemen, we must live through all time, or die by suicide. - Abraham Lincoln

I almost had a psychic girlfriend, but she left me before we met. - Steven Wright

I've been on a diet for two weeks and all I've lost is two weeks. - Totie Fields

The music business is a cruel and shallow money trench, a long plastic hallway where thieves and pimps run free, and good men die like dogs. There's also a negative side. - Hunter S. Thompson

I don't pay good wages because I have a lot of money; I have a lot of money because I pay good wages. - Robert Bosch

The only really good place to buy lumber is at a store where the lumber has already been cut and attached together in the form of furniture, finished, and put inside boxes. - Dave Barry

Happiness and misery are mental states. - Ramdas

Family isn't about whose blood you have. It's about who you care about. - Trey Parker and Matt Stone

When I was a boy I was told that anybody could become President; I'm beginning to believe it. - Clarence Darrow

A nation that continues year after year to spend more money on military defense than on programs of social uplift is approaching spiritual doom. - Martin Luther King Jr.

Men marry to make an end; women to make a beginning. - Alexis Dupuy

An actor is at most a poet and at least an entertainer. - Marlon Brando

When you stand for your liberty, we will stand with you. - George W. Bush

There is divinity in the selfless service to the suffering humanity.

What is now proved was once only imagined. - William Blake

Ernest Hemingway once wrote, 'The world is a fine place and worth fighting for,' I agree with the second part. - Morgan Freeman

War and conflicts begin in the minds of men, and peace, therefore, has to be established there.

Science is not about building a body of known 'facts.' It is a method for asking awkward questions and subjecting them to a reality check, thus avoiding the human tendency to believe whatever makes us feel good. - Terry Pratchett

I'm not sure how much movies should entertain. I've always been more interested in movies that scar. - David Fincher

A man may imagine things that are false, but he can only understand things that are true, for if the things be false, the apprehension of them is not understanding. - Isaac Newton

People who talk about the past are going backwards. People who talk about the present are maintaining. People who talk about the future are growing.

A judge is a law student who marks his own examination papers. - Henry Mencken

To sit alone with my conscience will be judgment enough for me. - Charles William Stubbs

It's not how old you are, it's how hard you work at it. - Jonah Barrington

Great men are they who see that spiritual force is stronger than material force, that thoughts rule the world.

Morality, like numinous awe, is a jump; in it, man goes beyond anything that can be 'given' in the facts of experience. - C.S. Lewis

I love argument, I love debate. I don't expect anyone just to sit there and agree with me, that's not their job. - Margaret Thatcher

Man climb to the highest summits but he cannot dwell there long - Bernard Shaw

Sitting at the table doesn't make you a diner, unless you eat some of what's on that plate. Being here in America doesn't make you an American. Being born here in America doesn't make you an American. - Malcolm X

If you have to forecast, forecast often. - Edgar R. Fiedler

I don't know half of you half as well as I should like; and I like less than half of you half as well as you deserve. - J.R.R. Tolkien

As I would not be a slave, so I would not be a master. This expresses my idea of democracy. Whatever differs from this, to the extent of the difference, is no democracy. - Abraham Lincoln

Few girls are as well shaped as a good horse. - Christopher Morley

Thanks to TV and for the convenience of TV, you can only be one of two kinds of human beings, either a liberal or a conservative. - Kurt Vonnegut

If opportunity doesn't knock, build a door. - Milton Berle

Talk to me about the truth of religion and I'll listen gladly. Talk to me about the duty of religion and I'll listen submissively. But don't come talking to me about the consolations of religion or I shall suspect that you don't understand. - C.S. Lewis

Motivation is the art of getting people to do what you want them to do because they want to do it. - Dwight D. Eisenhower

No man undertakes a trade he has not learned, yet everyone thinks of himself sufficiently qualified for that hardest of all trades - that of government – Socrates

God brings men into deep waters not to drown them, but to cleanse them – Aughey

We don't receive wisdom; we must discover it for ourselves after a journey that no one can take for us or spare us. - Marcel Proust

Just as your hand, held before the eye, can hide the tallest mountain, so this small earthly life keeps us from seeing the vast radiance that fills the core of the universe. - Nachman of Bratslav

Democracy is a form of government that substitutes election by the incompetent many for appointment by the corrupt few. - George Bernard Shaw

Ocean: A body of water occupying 2/3 of a world made for man...who has no gills. - Ambrose Bierce

If I must choose between righteousness and peace, I choose righteousness. - Theodore Roosevelt

Expect to win.

The louder he talked of his honor, the faster we counted our spoons. - Ralph Waldo Emerson

---

To live is so startling it leaves little time for anything else. - Emily Dickinson

---

Faith sees the invisible, believes the unbelievable and receives the impossible. - Corrie Ten Boom

---

Freedom is nothing else but a chance to be better. - Albert Camus

---

The trust of the innocent is the liar's most useful tool. - Stephen King

---

Until man duplicates a blade of grass, nature can laugh at his so-called scientific knowledge. - Thomas Edison

If you think a weakness can be turned into a strength, I hate to tell you this, but that's another weakness. - Jack Handey

When the president does it that means that it is not illegal. - Richard Nixon

Being responsible sometimes means pissing people off. - Colin Powell

Don't be reckless with other people's hearts, and don't put up with people that are reckless with yours. - Kurt Vonnegut

Courage is fear holding on a minute longer. - George Patton

I shall tell you a great secret my friend. Do not wait for the last judgment, it takes place every day. - Albert Camus

It is better to be alone than in bad company. - George Washington

Do more than is required. What is the distance between someone who achieves their goals consistently and those who spend their lives and careers merely following? The extra mile. - Gary Ryan Blair

A husband is what's left of the lover after the nerve has been extracted. - Socrates

For the want of a nail, the shoe was lost; for the want of a shoe the horse was lost; and for the want of a horse the rider was lost, being overtaken and slain by the enemy, all for the want of care about a horseshoe nail. - Benjamin Franklin

The greatest pleasure I know is to do a good action by stealth, and to have it found out by accident - Charles Lamb

He who loses money, loses much; He who loses a friend, loses much more, He who loses faith, loses all. - Eleanor Roosevelt

Life is a foreign language; all men mispronounce it. - Christopher Morley

If there were no God, there would be no Atheists. - GK Chesterton

---

When a friend is in trouble, don't annoy him by asking if there is anything you can do. Think up something appropriate and do it. - Edgar Watson Howe

---

If you can't feed a hundred people, then feed just one. - Mother Teresa

---

He who works hard achieves results. He works smarter achieves double the results.

Hitch your wagon to a star - Emerson

Children are innocent and love justice, while most adults are wicked and prefer mercy. - GK Chesterton

---

Without wearing any mask we are conscious of, we have a special face for each friend. - Oliver Wendell Holmes

---

I'm all in favor of keeping dangerous weapons out of the hands of fools. Let's start with typewriters. - Frank Lloyd Wright

---

To be a philosopher is not merely to have subtle thoughts; but so to love wisdom as to live according to its dictates. - Henry Thoreau

---

Walking with a friend in the dark is better than walking alone in the light. - Helen Keller

No matter how much cats fight, there always seem to be plenty of kittens. - Abraham Lincoln

A wise man gets more use from his enemies than a fool from his friends. - Baltasar Gracian

God plays purposefully; he created the Earth and the stones, so that we may learn stability from them.

I'm never going to be famous. My name will never be writ large on the roster of Those Who Do Things. I don't do anything. Not one single thing. I used to bite my nails, but I don't even do that anymore. - Dorothy Parker

People who like this sort of thing will find this the sort of thing they like. - Abraham Lincoln

We must use time as a tool, not as a crutch. - John F. Kennedy

---

Injustice anywhere is a threat to justice everywhere. - Martin Luther King Jr.

Civilization is the encouragement of differences. Civilization thus becomes a synonym of democracy. Force, violence, pressure, or compulsion with a view to conformity, is both uncivilized and undemocratic. - Mahatma Gandhi

---

You cannot go on 'explaining away' forever: you will find that you have explained explanation itself away. You cannot go on 'seeing through' things for ever. The whole point of seeing through something is to see something through it. - C.S. Lewis

---

Creativity is allowing yourself to make mistakes. Art is knowing which ones to keep. - Scott Adams

The time to repair the roof is when the sun is shining. - John F. Kennedy

All men are frauds. The only difference between them is that some admit it. I myself deny it. - Henry Mencken

Christmas can be celebrated in the school room with pine trees; tinsel and reindeers, but there must be no mention of the man whose birthday is being celebrated. One wonders how a teacher would answer if a student asked why it was called Christmas. - Ronald Reagan

A single death is a tragedy; a million deaths is a statistic. - Joseph Stalin

It would be fatal for the nation to overlook the urgency of the moment. This sweltering summer of the Negro's legitimate discontent will not pass until there is an invigorating autumn of freedom and equality. - Martin Luther King Jr.

We are faced with the paradoxical fact that education has become one of the chief obstacles to intelligence and freedom of thought. - Bertrand Russell

The fragrance always stays in the hand that gives the rose. - Hada Bejar

It is only our bad temper that we put down to being tired or worried or hungry; we put our good temper down to ourselves. - C.S. Lewis

I like the dreams of the future better than the history of the past. - Thomas Jefferson

To succeed, jump as quickly at opportunities as you do at conclusions. - Benjamin Franklin

The beginning is the most important part of the work. - Plato

The end of all knowledge must be building up of character - Mahatma Gandhi

True friends stab you in the front. - Oscar Wilde

———————⟋⟍⟍⟋———————

All men desire to know. - Aristotle

———————⟋⟍⟍⟋———————

Painting is just another way of keeping a diary. - Pablo Picasso

———————⟋⟍⟍⟋———————

How did it happen that their lips came together? How does it happen that birds sing, that snow melts, that the rose unfolds, that the dawn whitens behind the stark shapes of trees on the quivering summit of the hill? A kiss, and all was said. - Victor Hugo

———————⟋⟍⟍⟋———————

If the primary aim of a captain were to preserve his ship, he would keep it in port forever. - Thomas Aquinas

The poet is in command of his fantasy, while it is exactly the mark of the neurotic that he is possessed by his fantasy. - Lionel Trilling

We turn not older with years, but newer every day. - Emily Dickinson

Life's battles don't always go to the stronger or faster man. But sooner or later the man, who wins, is the man who thinks he can. - Vince Lombardi

Deep versed in books and shallow in himself. - Henry Kissinger

I want to thank everyone who made this night necessary. - Yogi Berra

I paid too much for it, but it's worth it. - Samuel
Goldwyn

Love lives by giving and forgiving. Self-lives by
getting and forgetting. Love is selflessness, self is
lovelessness.

Love lives by giving and forgiving. Self-lives by
getting and forgetting. Love is selflessness, self is
lovelessness.

The greatest thing in this world is not so much where
we are, but in what direction we are moving. - Oliver
Wendell Holmes

It is in vain to hope to please all alike. Let a man
stand with his face in what direction he will, he must
necessarily turn his back on one half of the world. -
George Dennison Prentice

As a woman, I find it very embarrassing to be in a meeting and realize I'm the only one in the room with balls. - Rita Mae Brown

Every year, back comes spring, with nasty little birds yapping their fool heads off and the ground all mucked up with plants. - Dorothy Parker

Man's nature is not always to advance; it has its advances and retreats. - Blaise Pascal
In giving, a man receives more than he gives, and the more is in proportion to the worth of the thing given. - George MacDonald

I am not young enough to know everything. - Oscar Wilde

Freedom is not something that anybody can be given;
freedom is something people take and people are as
free as they want to be. - James Baldwin

The true measure of a man is how he treats someone
who can do him absolutely no good. - Samuel
Johnson

Children need encouragement. So if a kid gets an
answer right, tell him it was a lucky guess. That way,
he develops a good, lucky feeling. - Jack Handey

God is like us to this extent, that whatever in us is
good is like God.

Impossible is a word to be found only in the
dictionary of fools. - Napoleon Bonaparte

For there is one thing we must never forget...the majority can never replace the man. And no if you want to achieve excellence, you can get there today. As of this second, quit doing less-than-excellent work - Thomas J Watson

He that cannot obey, cannot command. - Benjamin Franklin

Those who excel in virtue have the best right of all to rebel, but then they are of all men the least inclined to do so. - Aristotle

Experience is a dear teacher, but fools will learn at no other. - Benjamin Franklin

When calamity strikes one who is absent is saved.

There is no venom as sharp and strong as the venom of a tongue.

———————— ~~~ ————————

Creditors have better memories than debtors. - Benjamin Franklin

———————— ~~~ ————————

Beware of the man who works hard to learn something, learns it, and finds himself no wiser than before. He is full of murderous resentment of people who are ignorant without having come by their ignorance the hard way. - Kurt Vonnegut

———————— ~~~ ————————

Clever people seem not to feel the natural pleasure of bewilderment, and are always answering questions when the

———————— ~~~ ————————

Chief relish of a life is to go on asking them. - Frank Moore Colby

Experience is the teacher of all things. - Julius Caesar

If you are not living on the edge, you're taking up too much space.

An angry man is unfit to pray. - Nachman of Bratslav

It is easy to offer advice to others, but difficult to apply it to yourself.

The Goliath of totalitarianism will be brought down by the David of the microchip. - Ronald Reagan

You don't have to deserve your mother's love. You have to deserve your father's. - Robert Frost

Pride gets no pleasure out of having something, only out of having more of it than the next man. - C.S. Lewis

If there is anything that a man can do well, I say let him do it. Give him a chance. - Abraham Lincoln

Socialism is a philosophy of failure, the creed of ignorance, and the gospel or envy, its inherent virtue is the equal sharing of misery. - Winston Churchill

Whatever must happen ultimately should happen immediately. - Henry Kissinger

Iron rusts from disuse; stagnant water loses its purity and in cold weather becomes frozen; even so does inaction sap the vigor of the mind. - Leonardo da Vinci

To cease smoking is the easiest thing I ever did. I ought to know because I've done it a thousand times. - Mark Twain

---

I maintain that, if everyone knew what others said about him, there would not be four friends in the world. - Blaise Pascal

---

We need men who can dream of things that never were. - John F. Kennedy

---

It's called a pen. It's like a printer, hooked straight to my brain. - Dale Dauten

---

Every reader finds himself. The writer's work is merely a kind of optical instrument that makes it possible for the reader to discern what, without this book, he would perhaps never have seen in himself. - Marcel Proust

Never continue in a job you don't enjoy. If you're happy in what you're doing, you'll like yourself, you'll have inner peace. And if you have that, along with physical health, you will have had more success than you could possibly have imagined. - Johnny Carson

America is the first country to have gone from barbarism to decadence without the usual intervening period of civilization. - Oscar Wilde

Love is like a virus. It can happen to anybody at any time. - Maya Angelou

I don't want any yes-men around me. I want everybody to tell me the truth even if it costs them their jobs. - Samuel Goldwyn

Even the poor should give something to charity. - Nachman of Bratslav

Action may not always bring happiness; but there is no happiness without action - Benjamin Disraeli

One deceit needs many others, and so the whole house is built in the air and must soon come to the ground. - Baltasar Gracian

Marriage is the most natural state of man, and the state in which you will find solid happiness. - Benjamin Franklin

Success is simply a matter of luck. Ask any failure. - Earl Wilson

Just because I look sexy on the cover of Rolling Stone doesn't mean I'm naughty. - Britney Spears

It isn't enough to talk about peace. One must believe in it. And it isn't enough to believe in it. One must work at it. - Eleanor Roosevelt

We can only reason from what is; we can reason on actualities, but not on possibilities. - Thomas Paine

The task of the modern educator is not to cut down jungles, but to irrigate deserts. - C.S. Lewis

I care not what others think of what I do, but I care very much about what I think of what I do. That is character! - Theodore Roosevelt

You do what you are...You're born with a gift. If not that, then you get good at something along the way. And what you're good at you don't take for granted. - Morgan Freeman

Reasoning is never, like poetry, judged from the outside at all. - C.S. Lewis

I'm a great housekeeper: I get divorced, I keep the house. - Zsa Zsa Gabor

The time to take counsel of your fears is before you make an important battle decision. That's the time to listen to every fear you can imagine! When you have collected all the facts and fears and made your decision, turn off all your fears and go ahead. - George Patton

---

If the universe is so bad...how on earth did human beings ever come to attribute it to the activity of a wise and good Creator? - C.S. Lewis

---

Water, taken in moderation, cannot hurt anybody. - Mark Twain

---

Never give in--never, never, never, never, in nothing great or small, large or petty, never give in except to convictions of honor and good sense. Never yield to force; never yield to the apparently overwhelming might of the enemy. - Winston Churchill

If you want to know what God thinks of money, just look at the people he gave it to. - Dorothy Parker

———————～———————

Anger is one of the sinews of the soul; he that wants it hath a maimed mind. - Benjamin Franklin

———————～———————

Hitting is 50% above the shoulders. - Ted Williams

———————～———————

Knowledge is of two kinds. We know a subject ourselves, or we know where we can find information upon it. - Samuel Johnson

———————～———————

I get to go to lots of overseas places, like Canada. - Britney Spears

———————～———————

Realize how quickly time passes and you will plan better and achieve more.

―――――――――✦―――――――

It takes a lot of courage to show your dreams to someone else. - Erna Bombeck

―――――――――✦―――――――

For having lived long, I have experienced many instances of being obliged, by better information or fuller consideration, to change opinions, even on important subjects, which I once thought right but found to be otherwise. - Benjamin Franklin

―――――――――✦―――――――

One of the few good things about modern times: If you die horribly on television, you will not have died in vain. You will have entertained us. - Kurt Vonnegut

―――――――――✦―――――――

Anyone who says that they can contemplate quantum mechanics without becoming dizzy has not understood the concept in the least. - Niels Bohr

Never offend people with style when you can offend them with substance. - Sam Brown

For me, survival is the ability to cope with difficulties, with circumstances, and to overcome them. - Nelson Mandela

To command is to serve, nothing more and nothing less. - Andre Malraux

If you can't get them to salute when they should salute and wear the clothes you tell them to wear, how are you going to get them to die for their country? - George Patton

I don't generally feel anything until noon, and then it's time for my nap. - Oliver Wendell Holmes

If a pickpocket stands in a crowd of saints, all he sees are their pockets - Baba Hari Das

Religion is essentially the art and the theory of the remaking of man. Man is not a finished creation. - Edmund Burke

Providence and courage never abandon a good soldier

I have a hobby...I have the world's largest collection of sea shells. I keep it scattered on beaches all over the world. Maybe you've seen some of it... - Steven Wright

The real problem is not why some pious, humble, believing people suffer, but why some do not. - C.S. Lewis

You will become as small as your controlling desires; as great as your dominant aspirations.

If we command our wealth, we shall be rich and free; if our wealth commands us, we are poor indeed. - Edmund Burke

To waste, to destroy, our natural resources, to skin and exhaust the land instead of using it so as to increase its usefulness, will result in undermining in the days of our children the very prosperity which we ought by right to hand down to them. - Theodore Roosevelt

Vote for the man who promises least; he will be the least disappointing - Bernard Baruch

There is a remarkable breakdown of taste and intelligence at Christmas time. Mature, responsible grown men wear neckties made of holly leaves and drink alcoholic beverages with raw egg yolks and cottage cheese in them. - P.J. O'Rourke

Hell, there are no rules here - we're trying to accomplish something. - Thomas Edison

They say love is around every corner. I must be walking in circles.

Any fool can make things bigger, more complex, and more violent. It takes a touch of genius -- and a lot of courage -- to move in the opposite direction. - Albert Einstein

Political language is designed to make lies sound truthful and murder respectable, and to give an appearance of solidity to pure wind. - George Orwell

Diplomacy...the art of restraining power. - Henry Kissinger

Patience is something you admire in the driver behind you, but not in one ahead.

I'm like that guy who single-handedly built the rocket & flew to the moon! What was his name? Apollo Creed? - Homer Simpson

No side will win the Battle of the Sexes. There's too much fraternizing with the enemy. - Henry Kissinger

Money won't create success. The freedom to make it will. - Nelson Mandela

Genius thinks it can do whatever it sees others doing, but is sure to repent of every ill-judged outlay. - Johann Wolfgang von Goethe

It is hard to fail, but it is worse never to have tried to succeed. - Theodore Roosevelt

People demand freedom of speech to make up for the freedom of thought, which they avoid. - Soren Aabye Kierkegaard

---

It is in man's heart that the life of nature's spectacle exists; to see it, one must feel it. - Jean-Jacques Rousseau

---

Love at first sight is easy to understand; it's when two people have been looking at each other for a lifetime that it becomes a miracle. - Amy Bloom

---

Truth is the first causality in the game of politics.

Mind is a gold mine and a rubbish heap as well.

Informed decision-making comes from a long tradition of guessing and then blaming others for inadequate results. - Scott Adams

The world is governed more by appearances than realities, so that it is fully as necessary to seem to know something as to know it. - Daniel Webster

In our civilization, and under our republican form of government, intelligence is so highly honored that it is rewarded by exemption from the cares of office. - Ambrose Bierce

History is the version of past events that people have decided to agree upon. - Napoleon Bonaparte

Who will take medicine unless he knows he is in the grip of disease? - C.S. Lewis

The way to get things done is not to mind who gets the credit for doing them. - Benjamin Jowett

———————～———————

Keep dreaming big dreams. Who knows, maybe someday your dreams will come true so they might as well be big ones. - Gavin Sharples

———————～———————

You can tell a lot about a fellow's character by his way of eating jellybeans. - Ronald Reagan

———————～———————

If winning isn't everything, why do they keep score? - Vince Lombardi

———————～———————

Without music, life would be a mistake. - Friedrich Nietzsche

———————～———————

Be careful about reading health books. You may die of a misprint. - Mark Twain

Take time to love and be loved, for it is the greatest gift of life.

Having a male gynecologist is like going to an auto mechanic who doesn't own a car. - Carrie Snow

Anger as soon as fed is dead. It is starving that makes it fat. - Emily Dickinson

I am certainly not one of those who need to be prodded. In fact, if anything, I am the prod. - Winston Churchill

I'm not concerned about all hell breaking loose, but that a PART of hell will break loose... it'll be much harder to detect. - George Carlin

If men can develop weapons that are so terrifying as to make the thought of global war include almost a sentence for suicide, you would think that man's intelligence and his comprehension... would include also his ability to find a peaceful solution. - Dwight Eisenhower

It behooves every man to remember that the work of the critic is of altogether secondary importance, and that, in the end, progress is accomplished by the man who does things. - Theodore Roosevelt

Peace and justice are two sides of the same coin. - Dwight Eisenhower

Every poem can be considered in two ways--as what the poet has to say, and as a thing which he makes. - C.S. Lewis

Sports serve society by providing vivid examples of excellence. - George F. Will

Until you do what you believe in, how do you know whether you believe in it or not? - Leo Tolstoy

This will never be a civilized country until we expend more money for books than we do for chewing gum. - Elbert Hubbard

We know what happens to people who stay in the middle of the road. They get run over. - Ambrose Bierce

Every artist was first an amateur. - Ralph Waldo
Emerson

We must respect the other fellow's religion, but only
in the sense and to the extent that we respect his
theory that his wife is beautiful and his children are
smart. - Henry Mencken

It is not beauty that endears; its love that makes us
see beauty. - Leo Tolstoy

Why has government been instituted at all? Because
the passions of men will not conform to the dictates
of reason and justice, without constraint. - Alexander
Hamilton

Most new jobs won't come from our biggest employers; they will come from our smallest. We've got to do everything we can to make entrepreneurial dreams a reality - Ross Perot

---

Without losers, where would the winners be? - Casey Stengel

Think BIG and you will achieve BIG.

When the gods wish to punish us, they answer our prayers. - Oscar Wilde

---

They are able because they think so.

He who has not Christmas in his heart will never find it under a tree. - Roy L. Smith

Absence makes the heart grow fonder.

It made me sick to watch those businessmen applaud Welles during the 1975 AFI tribute, when you know that the next day if he asked any one of them for money, they'd say, 'We'll let you know.'" - John Cassavettes

A painter is a man who paints what he sells. An artist, however, is a man that sells what he paints. - Pablo Picasso

To be happy, you must learn to forget yourself.

If the United Nations once admits that international disputes can be settled by using force, then we will have destroyed the foundation of the organization and our best hope of establishing a world order. - Dwight Eisenhower

---

Is life so dear or peace so sweet as to be purchased at the price of chains and slavery? Forbid it, Almighty God! - Patrick Henry

---

The true aim of everyone who aspires to be a teacher should be, not to impart his own opinions, but to kindle minds.

A good book is the best of friends, the same to-day and forever. - Martin Farquhar Tupper

---

To announce that there must be no criticism of the president, or that we are to stand by the president right or wrong, is not only unpatriotic and servile, but is morally treasonable to the American public. - Theodore Roosevelt

And what's romance? Usually, a nice little tale where you have everything As You Like It, where rain never wets your jacket and gnats never bite your nose and it's always daisy-time. - D.H. Lawrence

If we have no peace, it is because we have forgotten that we belong to each other. - Mother Teresa

Pleasure is attained by fulfilling desire; happiness by overcoming it.

A stupid man's report of what a clever man says is never accurate because he unconsciously translates what he hears into something he can understand. - Bertrand Russell

The problem is not that we have too many fools; it's that the lightning isn't distributed right. - Mark Twain

Never look down on anybody unless you're helping them up. - Jesse Jackson

I do not want the peace that passeth understanding, I want the understanding that brings peace. - Helen Keller

Against criticism a man can neither protest nor defend himself; he must act in spite of it, and then it will gradually yield to him. - Johann Wolfgang von Goethe

Heaven offers nothing that a mercenary soul can desire. - C.S. Lewis

Persistence and determination alone are omnipotent. The slogan 'press on' has solved and always will solve the problems of the human race. - Calvin Coolidge

Life's most persistent and urgent question is, 'What are you doing for others?' - Martin Luther King Jr.

Special-interest publications should realize that if they are attracting enough advertising and readers to make a profit, the interest is not so special. - Fran Lebowitz

Progress is the activity of today and assurance of tomorrow - Emerson

The fool who has not sense to discriminate between what is good and what is bad is well-nigh as dangerous as the man who does discriminate and yet chooses the bad. - Theodore Roosevelt

Unless man is committed to the belief that all mankind are his brothers, then he labors in vain and hypocritically in the vineyards of equality. - Adam Clayton Powell Jr.

Every few seconds it changes - up an eighth, down an eighth -it's like playing a slot machine. I lose $20 million, I gain $20 million. - Ted Turner

---

Money is like a sixth sense without which you cannot make a complete use of the other five. - W. Somerset Maugham

---

Toleration is the best religion. - Victor Hugo

To cure the British disease with socialism was like trying to cure leukemia with leeches. - Margaret Thatcher

---

Abundance of money ruins the youth.

Then I look at the obituary page. If my name is not on it, I get up. - Benjamin Franklin

---

A good conscience is a continual Christmas. - Benjamin Franklin

---

The nice thing about being a celebrity is that, if you bore people, they think it's their fault. - Henry Kissinger

---

All great truths begin as blasphemies. - George Bernard Shaw

The law of compensation: What you sow, you will reap.

There is no friend as loyal as a book. - Ernest Hemingway

Age is a very high price to pay for maturity. - Tom Stoppard

I never knew what real happiness was until I got married, and by then it was too late. - Max Kaufman

---

In my heart, I think a woman has two choices: Either she's a feminist or a masochist. - Gloria Steinem

---

Many people mistake our work for our vocation. Our vocation is the love of Jesus. - Mother Teresa

---

The price good men pay for indifference to public affairs is to be ruled by evil men. - Plato

What we obtain too cheap, we esteem too lightly. - Thomas Paine

The people never give up their liberties but under some delusion. - Edmund Burke

Nothing that you have not given away will ever be really yours. - C.S. Lewis

The love we give away is the only love we keep. - Elbert Hubbard

Tell me what you eat, and I will tell you what you are. - Anthelme Brillat-Savarin

To be idle is a short road to death and to be diligent is a way of life; foolish people are idle, wise people are diligent. - Siddhartha Buddha

In wartime, truth is so precious that she should always be attended by a bodyguard of lies. - Winston Churchill

It is curious that physical courage should be so common in the world and moral courage so rare. - Mark Twain

Every act of creation is first of all an act of destruction. - Pablo Picasso

The movie's director is the pilot. It's his vision. For an actor, the time to worry about flying is when you're on the ground. If you don't want to fly with the director, don't get on the plane. - Denzel Washington

---

Ability will never catch up with the demand for it. - Confucius

---

War is a cowardly escape from the problems of peace. - Thomas Mann

---

Happiness does not come from doing easy work but from the afterglow of satisfaction that comes after the achievement of a difficult task that demanded our best. - Theodore Isaac Rubin

---

The recipe for perpetual ignorance is: be satisfied with your opinions and content with your knowledge. - Elbert Hubbard

Well done is better than well said. - Benjamin Franklin

So often we seek a change in our condition when what we need is a change in our attitude.

To find out a girl's faults, praise her to her girlfriends. - Benjamin Franklin

Our grand business undoubtedly is, not to see what lies dimly at a distance, but to do what lies clearly at hand.

When a politician is in opposition he is an expert on the means to some end; and when he is in office he is an expert on the obstacles to it. - GK Chesterton

What once was thought can never be unthought. - Friedrich Durrenmatt

Failures are divided into two classes - those who thought and never did, and those who did and never thought.

War - an act of violence whose object is to constrain the enemy, to accomplish our will. - George Washington

I'm not popular enough to be different. - Homer Simpson

A man only curses because he doesn't know the words to express what is on his mind. - Malcolm X

I discovered that rejections are not altogether a bad thing. They teach a writer to rely on his own judgment and to say in his heart of hearts, 'To hell with you.' - Saul Bellow

Women marry men hoping they will change. Men marry women hoping they will not. So each is inevitably disappointed. - Albert Einstein

No foreign policy - no matter how ingenious - has any chance of success if it is born in the minds of a few and carried in the hearts of none. - Henry Kissinger

It is better to starve than beg.

When people stop believing in God, they don't believe in nothing -- they believe in anything. - GK Chesterton

Be silent; if you have to talk, use words that are more powerful than silence - Swami Nirmalananda

The sole equality on earth is death. - Philip James Bailey

There is no service nobler than doing something nice for someone who will never find it out.

I don't know anything about music. In my line you don't have to. - Elvis Presley

Nothing worse could happen to one than to be completely understood. - Carl Jung

---

Our true nationality is mankind. - H.G. Wells

To err is not an error, but not to accept one's error is the error - Swami Nirmalananda

---

No matter what they're charging to get in, it's worth more to get out. - Roger Ebert

---

The trouble with the world is that the stupid are cocksure and the intelligent, full or doubt - Bertrand Russell

---

Of all the animals, man is the only one that lies. - Mark Twain

---

When you stop giving and offering something to the rest of the world, it's time to turn out the lights. - George Burns

---

Love is a canvas furnished by nature and embroidered by imagination. - Francois Marie Arouet (Voltaire)

Failure doesn't mean you are a failure it just means you haven't succeeded yet. - Robert H. Schuller

---

The best argument against democracy is a five-minute conversation with the average voter. - Winston Churchill

Find me a man who's interesting enough to have dinner with and I'll be happy. - Lauren Bacall

By three methods we may learn wisdom: First, by reflection, which is noblest; second, by imitation, which is easiest; and third by experience, which is the bitterest. - Confucius

It is better to offer no excuse than a bad one. - George Washington

It may be hard for an egg to turn into a bird: it would be a jolly sight harder for it to learn to fly while remaining an egg. We are like eggs at present. And you cannot go on indefinitely being just an ordinary, decent egg. We must be hatched or go bad. - C.S. Lewis

Sometimes people call me an idealist. Well, that is the way I know I am an American. America is the only idealistic nation in the world. - Woodrow Wilson

There is but one truly serious philosophical problem, and that is suicide. Judging whether life is or is not worth living amounts to answering the fundamental question of philosophy. - Albert Camus

Winning is not everything, but wanting to win is. - Vince Lombardi

There's so much comedy on television. Does that cause comedy in the streets? - Dick Cavett

Truth is sacred; and if you tell the truth too often nobody will believe it. - GK Chesterton

---

Love is the only force capable of transforming an enemy into friend. - Martin Luther King Jr.

I like long walks, especially when they are taken by people who annoy me. - Fred Allen

---

Life -- the way it really is -- is a battle not between bad and good but between bad and worse. - Joseph Brodsky

---

Happiness depends upon ourselves. - Aristotle

One who talks incessantly makes other bored.

Don't walk in front of me, I may not follow. Don't walk behind me, I may not lead. Just walk beside me and be my friend. - Albert Camus

---

I can live for two months on a good compliment. - Mark Twain

One should never trust a woman who tells her real age. If she tells that, she'll tell anything. - Oscar Wilde

---

Behind every successful man is a woman, behind her is his wife. - Groucho Marx

---

When a whole nation is roaring patriotism at the top of its voice, I am fain to explore the cleanness of its hands and purity of its heart. - Ralph Waldo Emerson

While I do not suggest that humanity will ever be able to dispense with its martyrs, I cannot avoid the suspicion that with a little more thought and a little less belief their number may be substantially reduced. - J.B.S. Haldane

Have the courage to say no. Have the courage to face the truth. Do the right thing because it is right. These are the magic keys to living your life with integrity. - W. Clement Stone

If you are obliged to neglect anything, let it be your chemistry. It is the least useful and the least amusing to a country gentleman of all the ordinary branches of science. - Thomas Jefferson

It is your mind that creates this world. - Siddhartha Buddha

A Canadian is someone who knows how to make love in a canoe. - Pierre Berton

We should not let our fears hold us back from pursuing our hopes. - John F. Kennedy

It is hard, if not impossible, to snub a beautiful woman - they remain beautiful and the rebuke recoils. - Winston Churchill

All are lunatics, but he who can analyze his delusions is called a philosopher. - Ambrose Bierce

There is nothing so absurd but some philosopher has said it. - Marcus Tullius Cicero

I honestly think it is better to be a failure at something you love than to be a success at something you hate. - George Burns

No amount of experimentation can ever prove me right; a single experiment can prove me wrong. - Albert Einstein

Journalism largely consists of saying 'Lord Jones is dead' to people who never knew that Lord Jones was alive. - GK Chesterton

I have from an early age abjured the use of meat, and the time will come when men will look upon the murder of animals as they now look upon the murder of men. - Leonardo da Vinci

It has been said that man is a rational animal. All my life I have been searching for evidence which could support this. - Bertrand Russell

Courtesy is as much a mark of a gentleman as courage. - Theodore Roosevelt

Airline travel is hours of boredom interrupted by moments of stark terror. - Al Boliska

No woman should ever be quite accurate about her age. It looks so calculating. - Oscar Wilde

A great many of those who 'debunk' traditional...values have in the background values of their own which they believe to be immune from the debunking process. - C.S. Lewis

I like to believe that people in the long run are going to do more to promote peace than our governments. Indeed, I think that people want peace so much that one of these days; governments had better get out of their way and let them have it. - Dwight Eisenhower

Opera is when a guy gets stabbed in the back and, instead of bleeding, he sings. - Ed Gardner

Suicide is man's way of telling God, 'You can't fire me - I quit.' - Bill Maher

Standing in the middle of the road is very dangerous;
you get knocked down by the traffic from both sides.
- Margaret Thatcher

If only for the sake of elegance, I try to remain
morally pure. - Marcel Proust

Don't pray when it rains if you don't pray when the
sun shines. - Satchel Paige

Anyone can dabble, but once you've made that
commitment, your blood has that particular thing in
it, and it's very hard for people to stop you. - Bill
Cosby

It ain't over till it's over. - Yogi Berra

For each illness that doctors cure with medicine, they provoke ten in healthy people by inoculating them with the virus that is a thousand times more powerful than any microbe: the idea that one is ill. - Marcel Proust

There is for each man, perfect self-expression. There is a place which he is to fill, some things he is to do, it is his destiny.

Every great decision creates ripples - like a huge boulder dropped in a lake. The ripples merge, rebound off the banks in unforeseeable ways. The heavier the decision, the larger the waves, the more uncertain the consequences. - Benjamin Disraeli

Without the aid of trained emotions the intellect is powerless against the animal organism. - C.S. Lewis

The greatest friend of Truth is time; her greatest enemy is Prejudice, and her constant companion Humility. - Charles Caleb Colton

Do not complain that the rose bush has thorns; rejoice that the thorn-bush bears roses.

Old age has deformities enough of its own. It should never add to them the deformity of vice. - Eleanor Roosevelt

The wise man always throws himself on the side of his assailants. It is more his interest than it is theirs to find his weak point. - Ralph Waldo Emerson

There is no man, however wise, who has not at some period of his youth said things, or lived in a way the consciousness of which is so unpleasant to him in later life that he would gladly, if he could, expunge it from his memory. - Marcel Proust

If you go on with this nuclear arms race, all you are going to do is make the rubble bounce. - Winston Churchill

When I study philosophical works I feel I am swallowing something which I don't have in my mouth. - Albert Einstein

What some call health, if purchased by perpetual anxiety about diet, isn't much better than tedious disease. - George Dennison Prentice

Nothing in the world is worth having or worth doing unless it means effort, pain, difficulty... I have never in my life envied a human being who led an easy life. I have envied a great many people who led difficult lives and led them well. - Theodore Roosevelt

You are not angry with people when you laugh at them. Humor teaches tolerance. - W. Somerset Maugham

The talent of success is nothing more than doing what you can do well, and doing well whatever you do without thought of fame. If it comes at all it will come because it is deserved, not because it is sought after. - Henry Wadsworth Longfellow

Punctuality is the thief of time. - Oscar Wilde

Both tears and sweat are salty, but they render a different result. Tears will get you sympathy; sweat will get you change. - Jesse Jackson

Character is that which reveals moral purpose, exposing the class of things a man chooses and avoids. - Aristotle

Think of God, constant contemplation of the Divine will free you from all worries - Baba

There has been only one Christmas - the rest are anniversaries. - W.J. Cameron

As the family goes, so goes the nation and so goes the whole world in which we live. - Pope John Paul II

To know what is impenetrable to us really exists, manifesting itself as the highest wisdom and the most radiant beauty...this knowledge; this feeling is at the center of true religiousness. - Albert Einstein

Dad always thought laughter was the best medicine, which I guess is why several of us died of tuberculosis. - Jack Handey

Reading without reflecting is like eating without digesting. - Edmund Burke

Mr. Gorbachev, open this gate! Mr. Gorbachev, tear down this wall! - Ronald Reagan

A kiss may ruin a human life. - Oscar Wilde

In the small matters trust the mind, in the large ones the heart. - Sigmund Freud

Undertake not what you cannot perform, but be careful to keep your promise - Washington

I don't believe in God because I don't believe in Mother Goose. - Clarence Darrow

People sleep peaceably in their beds at night only because rough men stand ready to do violence on their behalf. - George Orwell

Once you have flown, you will walk the earth with your eyes turned skywards, for there you have been, and there you long to return. - Leonardo da Vinci

There is no time for cut-and-dried monotony. There is time for work. And time for love. That leaves no other time! - Coco Chanel

Reason is our soul's left hand, Faith her right. - John Donne

I have come to the conclusion that my subjective account of my motivation is largely mythical on almost all occasions. I don't know why I do things. - J.B.S. Haldane

Opportunity is missed by most people, because it is dressed in overalls and looks like work. - Thomas Edison

Drama is life with the dull bits cut out. - Alfred Hitchcock

Have the strength of an elephant, the courage of a lion, the vigor of an oak and the purity of the Himalayan snow.

I feel impelled to speak today in a language that in a sense is new-one which I, who have spent so much of my life in the military profession, would have preferred never to use. That new language is the language of atomic warfare. - Dwight Eisenhower

The paradoxes of today are the prejudices of tomorrow, since the most benighted and the most deplorable prejudices have had their moment of novelty when fashion lent them its fragile grace. - Marcel Proust

Let us be thankful for the fools. But for them the rest of us could not succeed. - Mark Twain

Ignorance more frequently begets confidence than does knowledge: it is those who know little, and not those who know much, who so positively assert that this or that problem will never be solved by science. - Charles Darwin

———————～———————

The quality of a person's life is in direct proportion to their commitment to excellence, regardless of their chosen field of endeavor.

———————～———————

The greatest force in the world is thought.

———————～———————

The more corrupt the state, the more numerous the laws - Tactitus

———————～———————

Skill is successfully walking a tightrope over Niagara Falls. Intelligence is not trying.

If I feel physically as if the top of my head were taken off, I know that is poetry. - Emily Dickinson

The government consists of a gang of men exactly like you and me. They have, taking one with another, no special talent for the business of government; they have only a talent for getting and holding office. - Henry Mencken

Let him who desires peace prepare for war. - Vegetius

You know the only people who are always sure about the proper way to raise children? Those who've never had any. - Bill Cosby

We need true tax reform that will at least make a start toward restoring for our children the American Dream that wealth is denied to no one, that each individual has the right to fly as high as his strength and ability will take him. - Ronald Reagan

---

Truth never breaks, it breaks through.

A world without nuclear weapons would be less stable and more dangerous for all of us. - Margaret Thatcher

---

The only difference between death and taxes is that death doesn't get worse every time Congress meets. - Will Rogers

---

One must not always think so much about what one should do, but rather what one should be.

———— ～ ————

A mind of the caliber of mine cannot derive its nutriment from cows. - George Bernard Shaw

———— ～ ————

Simplicity is the ultimate sophistication. - Leonardo da Vinci

———— ～ ————

Today we can declare: Government is not the problem, and government is not the solution. We, the American people, we are the solution. - Bill Clinton

———— ～ ————

Friends have all things in common. - Plato

———— ～ ————

One definition of an economist is somebody who sees something happen in practice and wonders if it will work in theory. - Ronald Reagan

---

Children today are tyrants. They contradict their parents.

As soon as you trust yourself, you will know how to live. - Johann Wolfgang von Goethe

---

Pennies do not come from heaven. They have to be earned here on earth. - Margaret Thatcher

---

People who are not in love fail to understand how an intelligent man can suffer because of a very ordinary woman. This is like being surprised that anyone should be stricken with cholera because of a creature so insignificant as the comma bacillus. - Marcel Proust

I think 'no comment' is a splendid expression. I am using it again and again. - Winston Churchill

For a creative writer possession of the 'truth" is less important than emotional sincerity. - George Orwell

The meek shall inherit the Earth, but not its mineral rights. - J. Paul Getty

In the very books in which philosophers bid us scorn fame, they inscribe their names. - Marcus Tullius Cicero

The function of leadership is to produce more leaders, not more followers - Ralph Nader

Dance like nobody's watching; love like you've never been hurt. Sing like nobody's listening; live like it's heaven on earth. - Mark Twain

Better to die on your feet than live on your knees.

Where there is an open mind, there will always be a frontier. - Charles F. Kettering

It is a fine thing to establish one's own religion in one's heart, not to be dependent on tradition and second-hand ideals. Life will seem to you, later, not a lesser, but a greater thing. - D.H. Lawrence

The optimist sees the rose and not its thorns; the pessimist stares at the thorns oblivious of the rose - Kahlil Gibran

You must do the thing you think you cannot do. - Eleanor Roosevelt

If I read a book and it makes my whole body so cold no fire can ever warm me, I know that is poetry. - Emily Dickinson

The holy passion of Friendship is of so sweet and steady and loyal and enduring a nature that it will last through a whole lifetime, if not asked to lend money. - Mark Twain

When angry count to four; when very angry, swear. - Mark Twain

Our attitude towards others determines their attitude towards us. - Earl Nightingale

One swallow does not make a summer. - Aristotle

———————— ～ ————————

Practice economy, but do not be stingy.

———————— ～ ————————

The new rage is to say that the government is the cause of all our problems, and if only we had no government, we'd have no problems. I can tell you that contradicts evidence, history, and common sense. - Bill Clinton

———————— ～ ————————

Duty cannot exist without faith. - Benjamin Disraeli

———————— ～ ————————

Faith puts us in touch with infinite power, opens the way to unbounded possibilities, limitless achievements.

———————— ～ ————————

You can't wait for inspiration. You have to go after it with a club. - Jack London

The fact that a believer is happier than a skeptic is no more to the point than the fact that a drunken man is happier than a sober one. The happiness of credulity is a cheap and dangerous quality. - George Bernard Shaw

Success or failure in business is caused more by the mental attitude even than by mental capacities. - Walter Scott

If you want total security, go to prison. There you're fed, clothed, given medical care and so on. The only thing lacking... is freedom. - Dwight Eisenhower

Where love rules, there is no will to power; and where power predominates, there love is lacking. The one is the shadow of the other. - Carl Jung

I do not find in orthodox Christianity one redeeming feature. - Thomas Jefferson

As we look ahead into the next century, leaders will be those who empower others - Bill Gates

Creative force, like a musical composer, goes on unweariedly repeating a simple air or theme, now high, now low, in solo, in chorus, ten thousand times reverberated, till it fills earth and heaven with the chant. - Ralph Waldo Emerson

I take my wife everywhere, but she keeps finding her way back. - Henny Youngman

No man ever listened himself out of a job. - Calvin Coolidge

There are always two people in every picture: the photographer and the viewer. - Ansel Adams

The only kind of seafood I trust is the fish stick, a totally featureless fish that doesn't have eyeballs or fins. - Dave Barry

If you think there are no new frontiers, watch a boy ring the front doorbell on his first date. - Olin Miller

In a separation it is the one who is not really in love who says the more tender things. - Marcel Proust

All growth depends upon activity. There is no development physically or intellectually without effort, and effort means work. - Calvin Coolidge

The more often a man feels without acting, the less he'll be able to act. And in the long run, the less he'll be able to feel. - C.S. Lewis

Under democracy one party always devotes its chief energies to trying to prove that the other party is unfit to rule - and both commonly succeed, and are right. - Henry Mencken

It is better to have a permanent income than to be fascinating. - Oscar Wilde

If we could see the miracle of a single flower clearly, our whole life would change. - Siddhartha Buddha

I'm afraid that if you look at a thing long enough, it loses all of its meaning. - Andy Warhol

Puritanism - the haunting fear that someone, somewhere, may be happy. - Henry Mencken

Failures are finger posts on the road to achievement. - C.S. Lewis

It is not the place nor the condition, but the mind alone that can make anyone happy or miserable - L'Estrange

I wake each morning torn between the desire to improve the world and the desire to enjoy it. It makes it hard to plan the day. - E.B. White

In fact, just about all the major natural attractions you find in the West -- the Grand Canyon, the Badlands, the Goodlands, the Mediocrelands, the Rocky Mountains and Robert Redford -- were caused by erosion. - Dave Barry

If you know anything unworthy of a friend, forget it. If you know anything pleasant about the person, tell it.

Love is a growing, to full constant light; and his first minute, after noon, is night. - John Donne

Things work out best for those who make the best of how things work out - John Wooden

One day is lost if we have not laughed even once.

It is easier to forgive an enemy than to forgive a friend. - William Blake

Every act and event is the inevitable result of prior acts and events and is independent of human will. - Karl Marx

The American Republic will endure until the day Congress discovers that it can bribe the public with the public's money. - Alexis de Tocqueville

The Bible is not my book, and Christianity is not my religion. I could never give assent to the long, complicated statements of Christian dogma. - Abraham Lincoln

Whenever an individual or a business decides that success has been attained, progress stops. - Thomas J. Watson

Anger repressed can poison a relationship as surely as the cruelest words. - Dr. Joyce Brothers

Beautiful young people are accidents of nature, but beautiful old people are works of art. - Eleanor Roosevelt

The sleeping fox catches no poultry. - Benjamin Franklin

Snowboarding is an activity that is very popular with people who do not feel that regular skiing is lethal enough. - Dave Barry

Democracy is a device that ensures we shall be governed no better than we deserve. - George Bernard Shaw

You can observe a lot just by watching. - Yogi Berra

I generally avoid temptation unless I can't resist it. - Mae West

God cannot give us a happiness and peace apart from Himself, because it is not there. There is no such thing. - C.S. Lewis

Bodily exercise, when compulsory, does no harm to the body; but knowledge which is acquired under compulsion obtains no hold on the mind. - Plato

What the fool does at the end, the wise man does in the beginning. - Proverb

If we did not bring to the examinations of our instincts a knowledge of their comparative dignity, we could never learn it from them. - C.S. Lewis

When a man is able to take abuse with a smile, he is worthy to become a leader. - Nachman of Bratslav

I'm at an age where I think more about food than sex. Last week I put a mirror over my dining room table. - Rodney Dangerfield

A diplomat is a man who always remembers a woman's birthday but never remembers her age. - Robert Frost

Washington is a Hollywood for ugly people. Hollywood is a Washington for the simpleminded. - John McCain

Trouble shared is trouble halved. - Dorothy Sayers

It takes a great man to be a good listener. - Calvin Coolidge

There is time for everything. - Thomas Edison

From kindergarten to graduation, I went to public schools, and I know that they are a key to being sure that every child has a chance to succeed and to rise in the world. - Dick Cheney

I have just returned from Boston. It is the only sane thing to do if you find yourself up there. - Fred Allen

---

The customs and fashions of men change like leaves on the bough, some of which go and others come. - Dante Alighieri

---

A penny saved is a penny earned. - Benjamin Franklin

We all live with the objective of being happy; our lives are all different and yet the same.

What is art but a way of seeing? - Saul Bellow

You're never too old to become younger. - Mae West

Live as if you were to die tomorrow. Learn as if you were to live forever. - Mahatma Gandhi

---

A man can be short and dumpy and getting bald but if he has fire, women will like him. - Mae West

---

I think having land and not ruining it is the most beautiful art that anybody could ever want to own. - Andy Warhol

---

I have always thought that every woman should marry, and no man. - Benjamin Disraeli

---

My political ambitions have nothing to do with
vanity or the desire for power. I want to help people.
I owe them something after all they've done for me. -
Arnold Schwarzenegger

Yet each man kills the thing he loves, from all let this
be heard. Some does it with a bitter look, some with a
flattering word. The coward does it with a kiss the
brave man with the sword. - Oscar Wilde

Never ask pardon before you are accused.

Strong is the man who masters his will, stronger yet
is he who is mastered by his conscience.

Religion is fundamentally opposed to everything I hold in veneration - courage, clear thinking, honesty, fairness, and, above all, love of the truth. - Henry Mencken

If the new American father feels bewildered and even defeated, let him take comfort from the fact that whatever he does in any fathering situation has a fifty percent chance of being right. - Bill Cosby

Criticism is prejudice made plausible. - Henry Mencken

Happiness should always remain a bit incomplete. After all, dreams are boundless.

My idea of courage is the guy who has $500,000 tied up in the stock market and turns to the box scores first! - Earl Wilson

---

Of all the varieties of virtues, liberalism is the most beloved. - Aristotle

---

Imagination is a quality given a man to compensate him for what he is not, and a sense of humor was provided to console him for what he is. - Oscar Wilde

---

Sit in a quiet place, Relax the mind and body for a few minutes every day.

Happiness is a butterfly which, when pursued, is always just beyond your grasp but which, if you will sit down quietly, may alight upon you. - Nathaniel Hawthorne

Amassing wealth often ruins health.

Skiing combines outdoor fun with knocking down trees with your face. - Dave Barry

If a little dreaming is dangerous, the cure for it is not to dream less but to dream more, to dream all the time. - Marcel Proust

Religion operates not only on the vertical plane but also on the horizontal. It seeks not only to integrate men with God but to integrate men with men and each man with himself. - Martin Luther King Jr.

No great genius has ever existed without some touch of madness. - Aristotle

False words are not only evil in themselves, but they infect the soul with evil. - Plato

All virtue is summed up in dealing justly. - Aristotle

The greatest wealth is to live content with little. - Plato

Keep hope alive! - Jesse Jackson

My mother never saw the irony in calling me a son-of-a-bitch. - Jack Nicholson

We are all victims of mythology in one way or another. We are the inheritors, and many times the propagators, of a desire to believe what we want to believe, regardless of whether or not it is true. - J.V. Stewart

Time passes, and little by little everything that we have spoken in falsehood becomes true. - Marcel Proust

A wise man will make more opportunities than he finds. - Francis Bacon

A 'geek' by definition is someone who eats live animals....I've never eaten live animals. - Crispin Glover

I believe that unarmed truth and unconditional love will have the final word in reality. This is why right, temporarily defeated, is stronger than evil triumphant. - Martin Luther King Jr.

The ladder of success is best climbed by stepping on the rungs of opportunity. - Ayn Rand

In doubt a man of worth will trust to his own wisdom. - J.R.R. Tolkien

Not what we say about our blessings, but how we use them, is the true measure of our thanksgiving. - WT Purkiser

Between two groups of people who want to make inconsistent kinds of worlds, I see no remedy but force. - Oliver Wendell Holmes

There is only one success - to be able to spend your life in your own way. - Christopher Morley

Men talk of "finding God," but no wonder it is difficult; He is hidden in that darkest hiding-place, your heart. You yourself are a part of Him. - Christopher Morley

Courage is grace under pressure. - Ernest Hemingway

Associate yourself with men of good quality if you esteem your own reputation for it is better to be alone than in bad company.

The art of being happy lies in the power of extracting happiness from common things. - Henry Ward Beecher

Happiness is like a butterfly, if you chase it, it runs away; if you do not run after it, it will come rest on you.

The boundaries which divide life from death are at best shadowy and vague. Who shall say where the one ends, and where the other begins? - Edgar Allan Poe

Effort = Results.

What we have done for ourselves alone dies with us, what we have done for others and the world remains and is immortal.

If you're going to do something tonight that you'll be sorry for tomorrow morning, sleep late. - Henny Youngman

The art of acting consists in keeping people from coughing. - Benjamin Franklin

A grandmother pretends she doesn't know who you are on Halloween. - Erna Bombeck

Web users ultimately want to get at data quickly and easily. They don't care as much about attractive sites and pretty design. - Tim Berners-Lee

Man has almost constant occasion for the help of his brethren, and it is in vain for him to expect it from their benevolence only. - Adam Smith

Miracles are a retelling in small letters of the very same story which is written across the whole world in letters too large for some of us to see. - C.S. Lewis

I am my own experiment. I am my own work of art. - Madonna Ciccone

You can't buy love, but you can pay heavily for it. - Henny Youngman

I am not a has-been. I am a will be. - Lauren Bacall

We dare not forget that we are the heirs of that first revolution. - John F. Kennedy

It's going to be the ballot or the bullet. - Malcolm X

If you never take a chance, you will never be defeated, but you will never accomplish anything either.

There are three arts which are concerned with all things: one which uses, another which makes, and a third which imitates them. - Plato

Laughter is the sun that drives winter from the human face. - Victor Hugo

A bank is a place where they lend you an umbrella in fair weather and ask for it back when it begins to rain. - Robert Frost

If your business keeps you so busy that you have no time for anything else, there must be something wrong either with you or with your business. - William J. H. Boetcker

———～———

There is a force within that gives you life, seek that; in your body there lies a priceless jewel, seek that.

———～———

For two people in a marriage to live together day after day is unquestionably the one miracle the Vatican has overlooked. - Bill Cosby

———～———

A kind word rightly spoken, a smile or a cheer given to someone else quickly bounces back - G M Adams

———～———

A bare assertion is not necessarily the naked truth. - George Dennison Prentice

The fruit that can fall without shaking, indeed is too mellow for me. - Lady Mary Wortley Montagu

A film is - or should be - more like music than like fiction. It should be a progression of moods and feelings. The theme, what's behind the emotion, the meaning, all that comes later. - Stanley Kubrick

Nothing is wrong with Southern California that a rise in the ocean level wouldn't cure. - Kenneth Millar

The price of anything is the amount of life you exchange for it. - Henry Thoreau

We hate some persons because we do not know them; and we will not know them because we hate them. - Charles Caleb Colton

I believe in Christianity as I believe that the sun has risen, not only because I see it, but because by it I see everything else. - C.S. Lewis

---

Baseball is the belly-button of our society. - Bill Lee

A person with a new idea is a crank until the idea succeeds. - Mark Twain

---

External purity is achieved by water; internal purity will be evident by truthfulness - Tiruvalluvar

---

Being with a woman never hurt no professional ball player. It's staying up all night looking for a woman that does him in. - Casey Stengel

---

Love is the delightful interval between meeting a beautiful girl and discovering that she looks like a haddock. - John Barrymore

Beware the writer who always encloses the word reality in quotation marks: He's trying to slip something over on you. Or into you. - Edward Abbey

Those who believe they are exclusively in the right are generally those who achieve something. - Aldous Huxley

A cynic is a man who, when he smells flowers, looks around for a coffin. - Henry Mencken

Don't measure yourself by what you have accomplished, but by what you should have accomplished with your ability. - John Wooden

⸻

God enters by a private door into every individual. - Ralph Waldo Emerson

⸻

It is part of the American character to consider nothing as desperate - to surmount every difficulty by resolution and contrivance. - Thomas Jefferson

⸻

Let the river roll which way it will, cities will rise on its banks. - Ralph Waldo Emerson

⸻

The only paradise is paradise lost. - Marcel Proust

⸻

You are young, my son, and, as the years go by, time will change and even reverse many of your present opinions. Refrain therefore awhile from setting yourself up as a judge of the highest matters. - Plato

Liberty, when it begins to take root, is a plant of rapid growth. - George Washington

Those that despise people will never get the best out of others and themselves. - Alexis de Tocqueville

Beware of all enterprises that require new clothes. - Henry Thoreau

We must never be afraid to go too far, for success lies just beyond. - Marcel Proust

Books serve to show a man that those original thoughts of his aren't very new at all. - Abraham Lincoln

---

The government is best which governs least. - Thomas Jefferson

---

In this world there is always danger for those who are afraid of it. - George Bernard Shaw

---

Power is the ultimate aphrodisiac. - Henry Kissinger

We must learn to live together as brothers or perish together as fools. - Martin Luther King, Jr.

By working faithfully eight hours a day you may eventually get to be boss and work twelve hours a day. - Robert Frost

A pessimist sees the difficulty in every opportunity; an optimist sees the opportunity in every difficulty. - Winston Churchill

Our industries have expanded to such a point that they will burst their jackets if they cannot find a free outlet to the markets of the world. Our domestic markets no longer suffice. We need foreign markets. - Woodrow Wilson

The brain is a wonderful organ; it starts working the moment you get up in the morning and does not stop until you get into the office. - Robert Frost

Only those who are fit to live do not fear to die. And none are fit to die who have shrunk from the joy of life and the duty of life. Both life and death are parts of the same great adventure. - Theodore Roosevelt

When this girl at the museum asked me who I liked better, Monet or Manet, I said, 'I like mayonnaise.' She just stared at me, so I said it again, louder. Then she left. I guess she went to try to find some mayonnaise for me. - Jack Handey

The conviction of the rich that the poor are happier is no more foolish than the conviction of the poor that the rich are. - Mark Twain

America is a land of taxation that was founded to avoid taxation. - Laurence Peter

If my children wake up on Christmas morning and have someone to thank for putting candy in their stocking, have I no one to thank for putting two feet in mine? - GK Chesterton

It takes 20 years to build a reputation and five minutes to ruin it. If you think about that, you'll do things differently. - Warren Buffett

Part of the secret of success in life is to eat what you like and let the food fight it out inside. - Mark Twain

Skill without imagination is craftsmanship and gives us many useful objects such as wickerwork picnic baskets. Imagination without skill gives us modern art. - Tom Stoppard

Power over a man's subsistence is power over his will. - Alexander Hamilton

Everything that we see is a shadow cast by that which we do not see. - Martin Luther King Jr.

The trouble with fighting for human freedom is that one spends most of one's time defending scoundrels. For it is against scoundrels that oppressive laws are first aimed, and oppression must be stopped at the beginning if it is to be stopped at all. - Henry Mencken

Men do not differ much about what things they will call evils; they differ enormously about what evils they will call excusable. - GK Chesterton

True peace is not merely the absence of tension: it is the presence of justice. - Martin Luther King Jr.

There are two distinct classes of what are called thoughts: those that we produce in ourselves by reflection and the act of thinking and those that bolt into the mind of their own accord. - Thomas Paine

I know not with what weapons World War III will be fought, but World War IV will be fought with sticks and stones. - Albert Einstein

Now more than ever before, the people are responsible for the character of their Congress. If that body be ignorant, reckless and corrupt, it is because the people tolerate ignorance, recklessness and corruption. - James Garfield

Instead of burning a guy at the stake, what about burning him at the STILTS? It probably lasts longer, plus it moves around. - Jack Handey

———————〜〜———————

To have the reputation of possessing the most perfect social tact, talk to every woman as if you loved her, and to every man as if he bored you. - Oscar Wilde

———————〜〜———————

If you listen to your fears, you will die never knowing what a great person you might have been. - Robert H. Schuller

———————〜〜———————

Errors of haste are seldom committed singly. The first time a man always does too much. And precisely on that account he commits a second error, and then he does too little. - Friedrich Nietzsche

———————〜〜———————

There is no force so democratic as the force of an ideal. - Calvin Coolidge

Music is the wine that fills the cup of silence. - Robert Fripp

I wish I had a kryptonite cross, because then you could keep both Dracula and Superman away. - Jack Handey

Aging is mandatory. Maturity is optional. - Chris Antonak

Women have a thirst for order and beauty as for something physical; there is a strange female power of hating ugliness and waste as good men can only hate sin and bad men virtue. - GK Chesterton

A strict master will not have understanding sons. - Nachman of Bratslav

---

If you can build a business up big enough, it's respectable. - Will Rogers

---

Success in business requires training and discipline and hard work. But if you're not frightened by these things, the opportunities are just as great today as they ever were - David Rockefeller

---

It's a job that's never started that takes the longest to finish. - J.R.R. Tolkien

---

That is the true season of love, when we believe that we alone can love, that no one could ever have loved so before us, and that no one will love in the same way after us. - Johann Wolfgang von Goethe

Everyone's a pacifist between wars. It's like being a vegetarian between meals. - Colman McCarthy

———————～———————

Attitudes are contagious. Is yours worth catching?

———————～———————

God is a comedian playing to an audience too afraid to laugh. - Francois Marie Arouet (Voltaire)

———————～———————

For a time, at least, I was the most famous person in the entire world. - Jesse Owens

———————～———————

A man doesn't automatically get my respect. He has to get down in the dirt and beg for it. - Jack Handey

———————～———————

Trouble brings experience and experience brings wisdom.

———————— ∽ ————————

As government expands, liberty contracts. - Ronald Reagan

———————— ∽ ————————

Pulses and impulses both come from the heart. - Jason Mechalek

———————— ∽ ————————

It takes more than capital to swing business. You've got to have the A. I. D. degree to get by Advertising, Initiative, and Dynamics - Ren Mulford Jr.

———————— ∽ ————————

Our hope of immortality does not come from any religions, but nearly all religions come from that hope. - Robert G. Ingersoll

There is only one boss. The customer. And he can fire everybody in the company from the chairman on down, simply by spending his money somewhere else. - Sam Walton

There is no failure except in no longer trying. - Elbert Hubbard

Let us not forget that the cultivation of the earth is the most important labor of man. When tillage begins, other arts will follow. The farmers, therefore, are the founders of civilization. - Daniel Webster

It is vain to expect our prayers to be heard, if we do not strive as well as we pray - Aesop

Baseball and malaria keep coming back. - Gene Mauch

———————~———————

Humor is the most engaging cowardice. - Robert Frost

———————~———————

A happy life must be to a great extent a quiet life, for it is only in an atmosphere of quiet that true joy can live.

———————~———————

Call it a clan, call it a network, call it a tribe, and call it a family. Whatever you call it, whoever you are, you need one. - Jane Howard

———————~———————

Do not dwell in the past; do not dream of the future, concentrate the mind on the present moment. - Siddhartha Buddha

We are just an advanced breed of monkeys on a minor planet of a very average star. But we can understand the Universe. That makes us something very special. - Stephen Hawking

Voters don't decide issues; they decide who will decide issues. - George Will

The proper function of man is to live, not to exist.

Our natural, inalienable rights are now considered to be a dispensation from government, and freedom has never been so fragile, so close to slipping from our grasp as it is at this moment. - Ronald Reagan

What you have lost will not be returned to you. It will always be lost. You're left with only your scars to mark the void. All you can choose to do is go on or not. But if you go on, it's knowing you carry your scars with you. - Charles Frazier

Give a man a free hand and he'll run it all over you. - Mae West

A life without adventure is likely to be unsatisfying, but a life in which adventure is allowed to take whatever form it will is sure to be short. - Bertrand Russell

If you are really a product of a materialistic universe, how is it that you don't feel at home there? - C.S. Lewis

You do ill if you praise, but worse if you censure, what you do not understand. - Leonardo da Vinci

―――――――――〜―――――――

Nature is trying very hard to make us succeed, but nature does not depend on us. We are not the only experiment. - Buckminster Fuller

―――――――――〜―――――――

There is no expedient to which a man will not go to avoid the labor of thinking. - Thomas Edison

―――――――――〜―――――――

There is no more miserable human being than one in whom nothing is habitual except indecision - William James

―――――――――〜―――――――

Accept the challenges so that you can feel the exhilaration of victory. - George Patton

There are people who put their dreams in a little box and say, Yes, I've got dreams, of course I've got dreams. Then they put the box away and bring it out once in a while to look in it, and yep, they're still there. - Erna Bombeck

The West will not contain Communism, it will transcend Communism. We will not bother to denounce it; we'll dismiss it as a sad, bizarre chapter in human history whose last pages are even now being written. - Ronald Reagan

There is no kind of dishonesty into which otherwise good people more easily and frequently fall than that of defrauding the government. - Benjamin Franklin

Educations purpose is to replace an empty mind with an open one. - Malcolm Forbes

Whenever science makes a discovery, the devil grabs it while the angels are debating the best way to use it. - Alan Valentine

Traffic is like a bad dog. It isn't important to look both ways when crossing the street. It's more important to not show fear. - P.J. O'Rourke

Watch your words, watch your actions, watch your thoughts, watch your character, and watch your heart.

Men do not quit playing because they grow old; they grow old because they quit playing. - Oliver Wendell Holmes

If people don't come to the games, you can't stop them. - Yogi Berra

Familiarity breeds contempt - and children. - Mark Twain

———————～——————

Comedy is the art of making people laugh without making them puke. - Steve Martin

———————～——————

Disobedience, in the eyes of anyone who has read history, is man's original virtue. It is through disobedience that progress has been made, through disobedience and through rebellion. - Oscar Wilde

———————～——————

We need an America with the wisdom of experience. But we must not let America grow old in spirit. - Hubert H. Humphrey

———————～——————

Love never dies a natural death. It dies because we don't know how to replenish its source. It dies of blindness and errors and betrayals. It dies of illness and wounds; it dies of weariness, of witherings, of tarnishings. - Anais Nin

All our knowledge has its origin in our perceptions. - Leonardo da Vinci

The greatest happiness of life is the conviction that we are loved, loved for ourselves, or rather, loved in spite of ourselves. - Victor Hugo

It is unbecoming for young men to utter maxims. - Aristotle

It is difficult to be honest with oneself; it is much easier to be honest with other people.

A man who has never gone to school may steal from a freight car; but if he has a university education he may steal the whole railroad. - Theodore Roosevelt

Telling us to obey instinct is like telling us to obey 'people.' People say different things: so do instincts. Our instincts are at war. Each instinct, if you listen to it, will claim to be gratified at the expense of the rest. - C.S. Lewis

Never be afraid to try something new, professionals built the Titanic and Amateurs built the Ark.

Ambition is like a frog sitting on a Venus's-flytrap. The flytrap can bite and bite, but it won't bother the frog because it only has little tiny plant teeth. But some other stuff could happen and it could be like ambition. - Jack Handey

I am a soldier, I fight where I am told, and I win where I fight. - George Patton

Don't despair when the going gets rough, for that's when you discover how strong you really are.

I went into a restaurant and the sign said 'Breakfast anytime," so I ordered French toast during the Renaissance. - Steven Wright

Children seldom misquote you. In fact, they usually repeat word for word what you shouldn't have said.

A happy person is not a person in a special set of circumstances, but a person in a certain set of attitudes.

Better is a poor man living an honest life than a man of dishonest ways living being rich.

If world peace is our goal, we must stop all killing.

I am not judged by the number of times I fail, but by the number of times I succeed; and the number of times I succeed is in direct proportion to the number of times I can fail and keep on trying. - Tom Hopkins

---

Cast off the shackles of this modern oppression and take back what is rightfully yours, because as William Shakespeare never wrote, 'Life is but a bullring, and we are but matadors trying to dodge all the horns.' - Matthew Clayfield

---

America is a mistake, a giant mistake. - Sigmund Freud

Do something good for someone, somewhere.

Don't be "consistent" but be simply true. - Oliver Wendell Holmes

You must not fight too often with one enemy, or you will teach him all your art of war. - Napoleon Bonaparte

If you want to succeed you should strike out on new paths, rather than travel the worn paths of accepted success. - John Rockefeller

Man was made at the end of the week's work when God was tired. - Mark Twain

It is better to sleep on things beforehand than lie awake about them afterward. - Baltasar Gracian

Fortune knocks but once, but misfortune has much more patience. - Laurence Peter

The world cares very little about what a man or woman knows; it is what a man or woman is able to do that counts. - Booker T. Washington

Our contest is not only whether we ourselves shall be free, but whether there shall be left to mankind an asylum on earth for civil and religious liberty. - Samuel Adams

The main business of religions is to purify, control, and restrain that excessive and exclusive taste for well-being which men acquire in times of equality. - Alexis de Tocqueville

Men seldom make passes at girls who wear glasses. - Dorothy Parker

In life, as in art, the beautiful moves in curves. - Edward Bulwer-Lytton

Who likes not his business, his business likes not him. - William Hazlitt

The world is always ready to receive talent with open arms. Very often it does not know what to do with genius. - Oliver Wendell Holmes

First love is only a little foolishness and a lot of curiosity. - George Bernard Shaw

———————～———————

But what is the difference between literature and journalism? Journalism is unreadable and literature is not read. That is all. - Oscar Wilde

———————～———————

If a man empties his purse into his head, no one can take it from him. - Benjamin Franklin

———————～———————

Love is repaid by love alone! - Mother Teresa

———————～———————

It is not the going out of port, but the coming in, that determines the success of a voyage. - Henry Ward Beecher

———————～———————

Men occasionally stumble over the truth, but most of them pick themselves up and hurry off as if nothing happened. - Winston Churchill

No government can love a child, and no policy can substitute for a family's care. - Hillary Clinton

The curve is more powerful than the sword. - Mae West

The worst bankrupt in the world is the man who has lost his enthusiasm - H.W. Arnold

They always say time changes things, but you actually have to change them yourself. - Andy Warhol

Many receive advice, only the wise profit by it - Syrus

Science may set limits to knowledge, but should not set limits to imagination. - Bertrand Russell

---

He does not possess wealth; it possesses him. - Benjamin Franklin

---

The secret to staying young is to live honestly, eat slowly, and lie about your age. - Lucille Ball

---

Just the omission of Jane Austen's books alone would make a fairly good library out of a library that hadn't a book in it. - Mark Twain

---

Woman begins by resisting a man's advances and ends by blocking his retreat. - Oscar Wilde

The doors of wisdom are never shut. - Benjamin Franklin

By paying too much attention to other's faults we die before having had the time to know our own - La Bruyere

The mintage of wisdom is to know that rest is rust, and that real life is in love, laughter, and work. - Elbert Hubbard

Marriage is a duel to the death which no man of honor should decline. - GK Chesterton

The spirit of resistance to government is so valuable on certain occasions that I wish it to be always kept alive. It will often be exercised when wrong, but better so than not to be exercised at all. - Thomas Jefferson

From the moment I picked your book up until I laid it down I was convulsed with laughter. Someday I intend reading it. - Groucho Marx

Journalism is literature in a hurry. - Matthew Arnold

The secret of success in life is for a man to be ready for his opportunity when it comes. - Benjamin Disraeli

I think it's the duty of the comedian to find out where the line is drawn and cross it deliberately. - George Carlin

Men never do evil so completely and cheerfully as when they do it from religious conviction. - Blaise Pascal

I have an existential map; it has 'you are here' written all over it. - Steven Wright

The biggest risk is not taking one.

Whenever a thing is done for the first time, it releases a little demon. - Emily Dickinson

Prayer, if not the very gate of heaven, is the key to let us info its holiness and joys.

What's the subject of life - to get rich? All of those fellows out there getting rich could be dancing around the real subject of life. - Paul A. Volcker

Whatever your mind can conceive and believe it CAN achieve.

Being a philosopher, I have a problem for every solution. - Robert Zend

When you are arguing against Him you are arguing against the very power that makes you able to argue at all. - C.S. Lewis

The caliber of a person is to be found in the ability to meet disappointment and be enriched rather than embittered by it.

If you can't dazzle them with brilliance, baffle them with bull. - W.C. Fields

Take from the church the miraculous, the supernatural, the incomprehensible, the unreasonable, the impossible, the unknowable, the absurd, and nothing but a vacuum remains. - Robert G. Ingersoll

If a person with multiple personalities threatens suicide, is that considered a hostage situation? - Steven Wright

Celebrate the blessings of God and praise him for his kindness towards you, thank him for his previous gifts.

In every weak person there is a strong human being. In every evil human being is a good person. In every defeated person there is a victorious one. To become aware of this nobility and power within ourselves is the greatest discovery - S. Perry

Men take more pains to mask than mend - Benjamin Franklin

Intoxicated with unbroken success, we have become too self-sufficient to feel the necessity of redeeming and preserving grace, too proud to pray to the God that made us. - Abraham Lincoln

When I was younger I could remember anything, whether it happened or not. - Mark Twain

———— ～～ ————

The healthy man does not torture others - generally it is the tortured who turn into torturers. - Carl Jung

———— ～～ ————

If we discovered that we only had five minutes left to say all that we wanted to say, every telephone booth would be occupied by people calling other people to stammer that they loved them. - Christopher Morley

———— ～～ ————

The only defensible war is a war of defense. - GK Chesterton

———— ～～ ————

Today's students can put dope in their veins or hope in their brains. If they can conceive it and believe it, they can achieve it. They must know it is not their aptitude, but their attitude, that will determine their altitude. - Jesse Jackson

I never forget a face, but in your case I'll be glad to make an exception. - Groucho Marx

Theology is only thought applied to religion. - GK Chesterton

A poem begins in delight and ends in wisdom. - Robert Frost

University politics are vicious precisely because the stakes are so small. - Henry Kissinger

Deliberate with caution, but act with decision; and yield with graciousness, or oppose with firmness. - Charles Caleb Colton

I'd rather earn 1% from 100 people's effort than 100% from my own efforts. - John P Getty

Maturity is a bitter disappointment for which no remedy exists, unless laughter can be said to remedy anything. - Kurt Vonnegut

God is more truly imagined than expressed, and He exists more truly than He is imagined. - Saint Augustine

Actors are one family over the entire world. - Eleanor Roosevelt

Too much capitalism does not mean too many capitalists, but too few capitalists. - GK Chesterton

---

When you have to kill a man, it costs nothing to be polite. - Winston Churchill

---

After 'The Matrix,' I cannot wear sunglasses. As soon as I put them on, people recognize me. - Carrie-Anne Moss

---

It does not do to dwell on dreams and forget to live. - J.K. Rowling

---

The absent are easily refuted. - C.S. Lewis

Whoever cares to learn will always find a teacher.

When people hear good music, it makes them homesick for something they never had and never will have. - Edgar Watson Howe

---

Keep a note pad and pencil on your bedside table. Million dollar ideas sometimes strike at 3 am - H Jackson Brown Jnr

---

Slump? I ain't in no slump... I just ain't hitting. - Yogi Berra

---

The usual approach of science of constructing a mathematical model cannot answer the questions of why there should be a universe for the model to describe. Why does the universe go to all the bother of existing? - Stephen Hawking

The artist is nothing without the gift, but the gift is nothing without work. - Emile Zola

---

The last temptation is the greatest treason: to do the right deed for the wrong reason. - T.S. Eliot

---

I can think of nothing more boring for the American people than to have to sit in their living rooms for a whole half hour looking at my face on their television screens. - Dwight Eisenhower

---

With the sleep of dreams come nightmares. - William Shakespeare

---

Badness is only spoiled goodness. - C.S. Lewis

Plough deep while sluggards sleep. - Benjamin
Franklin

Physics is like sex: sure, it may give some practical
results, but that's not why we do it. - Richard P.
Feynman

TV is chewing gum for the eyes. - Frank Lloyd
Wright

Democracy is the theory that the common people
know what they want and deserve to get it good and
hard. - Henry Mencken

Philosophical argument has sometimes shaken my
reason for the faith that was in me; but my heart has
always assured me that the Gospel of Jesus Christ
must be reality. - Daniel Webster

Proverbs are always platitudes until you have personally experienced the truth of them. - Aldous Huxley

You make 'em, I amuse 'em. - Theodor Seuss Geisel

Things are more like they are today than they have ever been before. - Dwight Eisenhower

Childbirth, as a strictly physical phenomenon, is comparable to driving a United Parcel truck through an inner tube. - Dave Barry

If we will not learn to eat the only food that the universe grows...then we must starve eternally. - C.S. Lewis

I've got all the money I'll ever need, if I die by four o'clock. - Henny Youngman

The absence of alternatives clears the mind marvelously. - Henry Kissinger

The person who runs away exposes himself to that very danger more than a person who sits quietly.

Not for nothing is their motto TGIF - 'Thank God It's Friday.' They live for the weekends, when they can go do what they really want to do. - Richard Nelson Bolles

No one is guaranteed happiness. Life just gives each person time and space. It is up to us to fill it with joy.

Freedom is hammered out on the anvil of discussion, dissent, and debate. - Hubert H. Humphrey

The reason I love my dog so much is because when I come home, he's the only one in the world who treats me like I'm The Beatles. - Bill Maher

As a rule, men worry more about what they can't see than about what they can. - Julius Caesar

Ridicule is generally made use of to laugh men out of virtue and good sense, by attacking everything praiseworthy in human life. - Joseph Addison

If god is to live in us, pride must die - Dr. S Radhakrishna

My aim is to put down on paper what I see and what I feel in the best and simplest way. - Ernest Hemingway

Many books require no thought from those who read them, and for a very simple reason; they made no such demand upon those who wrote them. - Charles Caleb Colton

If we knew what it was we were doing, it would not be called research, would it? - Albert Einstein

To succeed, we must first believe that we can. - Michael Korda

If I cannot horrify, I'll go for the gross-out. I'm not proud. - Stephen King

Happiness is not a goal; it is a by-product. - Eleanor Roosevelt

———————～———————

How selfish so ever man may be supposed, there are evidently some principles in his nature, which interest him in the fortune of others, and render their happiness necessary to him, though he derives nothing from it, except the pleasure of seeing it. - Adam Smith

———————～———————

God gave us two ends. One to sit on and one to think with. Success depends on which one you use; head you win, tail, you lose.

———————～———————

Make good decisions and you'll succeed, make bad ones and you'll fail. - Gary Kasparov

———————～———————

I think vital religion has always suffered when orthodoxy is more regarded than virtue. The scriptures assure me that at the last day we shall not be examined on what we thought but what we did. - Benjamin Franklin

Christmas is not a time nor a season, but a state of mind. To cherish peace and goodwill, to be plenteous in mercy, is to have the real spirit of Christmas. - Calvin Coolidge

Don't simply retire from something; have something to retire to. - Harry Emerson Fosdick

When you see a good man think of following him; when you see a bad one, examine your own heart.

I wish I had an answer to that, because I'm tired of answering that question. - Yogi Berra

---

The opposite of talking isn't listening. The opposite of talking is waiting. - Fran Lebowitz

---

Let individuals contribute as they desire; but let us prohibit in effective fashion all corporations from making contributions for any political purpose, directly or indirectly. - Theodore Roosevelt

---

A true artist will let his wife starve; his children go barefoot, his mother drudge for his living at seventy, sooner than work at anything but his art. - George Bernard Shaw

---

God is really only another artist. He invented the giraffe, the elephant and the cat. He has no real style; He just goes on trying other things. - Pablo Picasso

Do not needlessly endanger your lives until I give you the signal. - Dwight Eisenhower

There is a tragic flaw in our precious Constitution, and I don't know what can be done to fix it. This is it: Only nut cases want to be president. - Kurt Vonnegut

In an atmosphere of liberty, artists and patrons are free to think the unthinkable and create the audacious; they are free to make both horrendous mistakes and glorious celebrations. - Ronald Reagan

There is one thing alone that stands the brunt of life throughout its course: a quiet conscience. - Euripides

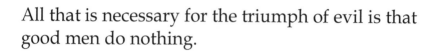

All that is necessary for the triumph of evil is that good men do nothing.

Consumption is the sole end and purpose of all production; and the interest of the producer ought to be attended to, only so far as it may be necessary for promoting that of the consumer. - Adam Smith

A government which robs Peter to pay Paul can always depend on the support of Paul. - George Bernard Shaw

The truly great are those who willingly recognize their own deficiencies.
I'd just as soon play tennis with the net down. - Robert Frost

The U.S. Constitution doesn't guarantee happiness, only the pursuit of it. You have to catch up with it yourself. - Benjamin Franklin

All men are timid on entering any fight. Whether it is the first or the last fight, all of us are timid. Cowards are those who let their timidity get the better of their manhood. - George Patton

The most important things are the hardest things to say. They are the things you get ashamed of because words diminish your feelings - words shrink things that seem timeless when they are in your head to no more than living size when they are brought out. - Stephen King

Elderly men who are popular with young women usually lack wisdom. - Nachman of Bratslav

No man is an island; every man is a piece of the continent, a part of the main.

———————

A man always has two reasons for doing anything – a good reason and the real reason – J. P. Morgan

———————

Liberty has never come from the government. Liberty has always come from the subjects of it. The history of liberty is a history of resistance. - Woodrow Wilson

———————

Film lovers are sick people. - Francois Truffaut

———————

When you become senile, you won't know it. - Bill Cosby

———————

The true meaning of life is to plant trees, whose shade you do not expect to sit. - Nelson Henderson

The people who get on in this world are the people who get up and look for the circumstances they want and if they can't find them, make them. - George Bernard Shaw

Ultimately the bond of all companionship, whether in marriage or in friendship, is conversation. - Oscar Wilde

Animals are my friends... and I don't eat my friends. - George Bernard Shaw

Be faithful in small things because it is in them that your strength lies. - Mother Teressa

For in the final analysis, our most basic common link, is that we all inhabit this small planet, we all breathe the same air, we all cherish our children's futures, and we are all mortal. - John F. Kennedy

Remember if you marry for beauty, thou bindest thyself all thy life for that which perchance, will neither last nor please thee one year: and when thou hast it, it will be to thee of no price at all. - Emily Dickinson

It is not length of life, but depth of life. - Ralph Waldo Emerson

A successful marriage is an edifice that must be rebuilt every day. - André Maurois

Men's minds are raised to the level of the women with whom they associate. - Alexandre Dumas

The flowers anew, returning seasons bring! But beauty faded has no second spring. - Frank Moore Colby

Men acquire a particular quality by constantly acting in a particular way. - Aristotle

If you realize you were wrong, have the courage to admit it - Swami Chinmayananda

Ambition is pitiless. Any merit that it cannot use it finds despicable. - Eleanor Roosevelt

A single lie destroys a whole reputation of integrity. - Baltasar Gracian

---

Knowledge that is paid for will be longer remembered. - Nachman of Bratslav

---

We will have to repent in this generation not merely for the hateful words and actions of the bad people but for the appalling silence of the good people. - Martin Luther King Jr.

Happiness and moral duty are inseparably connected. - George Washington

---

Happiness is a Swedish sunset; it is there for all, but most of us look the other way and lose it. - Mark Twain

We live in deeds, not years: In thoughts not breaths; in feelings, not in figures on a dial. We should count time by heart throbs. He most lives who thinks most, feels the noblest, and acts the best. - Aristotle

There was a time when a fool and his money were soon parted, but now it happens to everybody. - Adlai E. Stevenson

If you have a job without aggravation, you don't have a job. - Malcolm Forbes

Writing is the only thing that, when I do it, I don't feel I should be doing something else. - Gloria Steinem

I'm not afraid of death; I just don't want to be there when it happens. - Woody Allen

Always forgive your enemies; nothing annoys them so much. - Oscar Wilde

Don't marry a man to reform him - that's what reform schools are for. - Mae West

Knowledge speaks, but wisdom listens. - Jimi Hendrix

Diligence is the mother of good luck. - Benjamin Franklin

Don't knock the weather; nine-tenths of the people couldn't start a conversation if it didn't change once in a while. - Kin Hubbard

The genius of democracies is seen not only in the great number of new words introduced but even more in the new ideas they express. - Alexis de Tocqueville

Peace is not merely a distant goal that we seek, but a means by which we arrive at that goal. - Martin Luther King Jr.

It is a terrible thing to see and have no vision. - Helen Keller

What happens if a big asteroid hits Earth? Judging from realistic simulations involving a sledge hammer and a common laboratory frog, we can assume it will be pretty bad. - Dave Barry

Music takes us out of the actual and whispers to us dim secrets that startle our wonder as to who we are, and for what, whence, and whereto. - Ralph Waldo Emerson

Never murder a man who is committing suicide. - Woodrow Wilson

Anyone who stops learning is old, whether at twenty or eighty. Anyone who keeps learning stays young. The greatest thing in life is to keep your mind young. - Henry Ford

America is a nation with many flaws, but hopes so vast that only the cowardly would refuse to acknowledge them. - James Michener

Go as far as you can see; when you get there, you will be able to see farther – J.P. Morgan

Too many poets delude themselves by thinking that the mind is dangerous and must be left out. Well, the mind is dangerous and must be left in. - Robert Frost

It is only by labor that thought can be made healthy, and only by thought that labor can be made happy.

How do you tell a Communist? Well, it's someone who reads Marx and Lenin. And how do you tell an anti-Communist? It's someone who understands Marx and Lenin. - Ronald Reagan

It is not a matter of what is true that counts, but a matter of what is perceived to be true. - Henry Kissinger

Vision + Sacrifice + Patience = SUCCESS.

Keep your view point broad and generous.

There is nothing more exhilarating than to be shot at without result. - Winston Churchill

Swallow your pride occasionally, it's not fattening. - Frank Tyger

Nobody in football should be called a genius. A genius is a guy like Norman Einstein. - Joe Theismann

When an idea exclusively occupies the mind, it is transformed into an actual physical or mental state – Swami Vivekananda

What is it that makes a complete stranger dive into an icy river to save a solid-gold baby? Maybe we'll never know. - Jack Handey

Sincerity is to speak as we think, to perform what we promise, and really to be what we would seem and appear to be.

I cannot undertake to lay my finger on that article of the Constitution which granted a right to Congress of expending, on the objects of benevolence, the money of their constituents. - James Madison

When you have a problem convert it into a challenge for problems worry you and challenges inspire you.

In the arts of life man invents nothing; but in the arts of death he outdoes Nature herself, and produces by chemistry and machinery all the slaughter of plague, pestilence, and famine. - George Bernard Shaw

---

If it weren't for Philo T. Farnsworth, inventor of television, we'd still be eating frozen radio dinners. - Johnny Carson

---

The only rock I know that stays steady, the only institution I know that works is the family. - Lee Iacocca

---

Outside of its legitimate function, government does nothing as well or as economically as the private sector. - Ronald Reagan

There is a miracle that men can love God, yet fail to love humanity. With whom are they in love then? - Sri Aurobindo

The miracle is not that we do this work, but that we are happy to do it. - Mother Teresa

Instead of loving people and using things, we love things and use people.

The supreme spiritual law is that health, harmony and happiness are directly dependent upon right thinking.

A friendship founded on business is a good deal better than a business founded on friendship - John D Rockerfeller

———————～———————

We are shut up in schools and college recitation rooms for ten or fifteen years, and come out at last with a bellyful of words and do not know a thing. - Ralph Waldo Emerson

———————～———————

Cocaine is God's way of telling someone that they're too rich. - Robin Williams

———————～———————

You cannot believe in God until you believe in yourself – Swami Vivekananda

———————～———————

To think is to differ. - Clarence Darrow

Force and strife work upon the passions and fears, but love and peace reach and reform the heart.

A friend is the hope of the heart. - Ralph Waldo Emerson

As I grow older, I pay less attention to what men say. I just watch what they do. - Andrew Carnegie

---

I hate it when my leg falls sleep in the middle of the day, because that means it'll be up all night. - Steven Wright

---

Skepticism is a virtue in history as well as in philosophy. - Napoleon Bonaparte

---

The man who disobeys his parents will have disobedient sons. - Nachman of Bratslav

---

Since love grows within you, so beauty grows. For love is the beauty of the soul. - Saint Augustine

---

Don't overestimate the decency of the human race. - H. L. Mencken

---

Giving is the highest level of living. - John C Maxwell

It was when I was happiest that I longed most...The sweetest thing in all my life has been the longing...to find the place where all the beauty came from. - C.S. Lewis

Music is a moral law. It gives soul to the universe, wings to the mind, flight to the imagination, and charm and gaiety to life and to everything. - Plato

Corporation: An ingenious device for obtaining profit without individual responsibility. - Ambrose Bierce

It is hard to believe that a man is telling the truth when you know that you would lie if you were in his place. - Henry Mencken

When you get to the end of your rope, tie a knot and hang on. - Franklin D. Roosevelt

You're entitled to your own opinion, but not your own facts.

Change is inevitable. Change is constant. - Benjamin Disraeli

Trust because you are willing to accept the risk, not because it's safe or certain.

The pebbl'd shore, so do our minutes hasten to their end. - William Shakespeare

To be a poet is a condition, not a profession. - Robert Frost

He has all the virtues I dislike and none of the vices I admire. - Winston Churchill

This above all: to thine own self be true, and it must follow, as the night the day, thou canst not then be false to any man. - William Shakespeare

The sports page records people's accomplishments; the front page nothing but their failures. - Earl Warren

A wise man will make more opportunities than he finds. - Francis Bacon

Anyone who is not an anarchist agrees with having a policeman at the corner of the street; but the danger at present is that of finding the policeman half-way down the chimney or even under the bed. - GK Chesterton

The genius of a good leader is to leave behind him a situation which common sense, without the grace of genius, can deal with successfully. - Walter Lippmann

---

Music is a safe kind of high. - Jimi Hendrix

Going into business for yourself, becoming an entrepreneur, is the modern-day equivalent of pioneering on the old frontier - Paula Nelson

---

There is one thing I would break up over, and that is if she caught me with another woman. I won't stand for that. - Steve Martin

---

Love yourself first and everything else falls into line. You really have to love yourself to get anything done in this world. - Lucille Ball

The two most beautiful words in the English language are 'check enclosed.' - Dorothy Parker

I believe that the next half century will determine if we will advance the cause of Christian civilization or revert to the horrors of brutal paganism. - Theodore Roosevelt

If one does not understand a person, one tends to regard him as a fool. - Carl Jung

A second marriage is the triumph of hope over experience. - Samuel Johnson

To teach how to live with uncertainty, yet without being paralyzed by hesitation, is perhaps the chief thing that philosophy can do. - Bertrand Russell

There never was yet a truly great man that was not at the same time truly virtuous - Benjamin Franklin

---

Art is the lie that tells the truth. - Pablo Picasso

If variety is the spice of life, marriage is the big can of leftover Spam. - Johnny Carson

---

In the middle of every difficulty lies opportunity. - Albert Einstein

---

Life is pleasant. Death is peaceful. It's the transition that's troublesome. - Jimi Hendrix

---

The Law of conservation of energy tells us we can't get something for nothing, but we refuse to believe it. - Isaac Asimov

---

If my critics saw me walking over the Thames they would say it was because I couldn't swim. - Margaret Thatcher

---

The essence of romantic love is not the company of a lover but the pursuit. - Andrew Sullivan

---

Inspiration exists, but it has to find you working. - Pablo Picasso

---

The taxpayers are sending congressmen on expensive trips abroad. It might be worth it except they keep coming back. - Will Rogers

The surprising thing about young fools is how many survive to become old fools. - Doug Larson

Science is a first-rate piece of furniture for a man's upper chamber, if he has common sense on the ground floor. - Oliver Wendell Holmes

Patience is the companion of wisdom. - Saint Augustine

A successful marriage requires falling in love many times, always with the same person. - Germaine Greer

People are definitely a company's greatest asset. It doesn't make any difference whether the product is cars or cosmetics. A company is only as good as the people it keeps - Mary Kay Ash

The battle is now joined on many fronts. We will not waver; we will not tire; we will not falter; and we will not fail. - George W. Bush

If you're given a choice between money and sex appeal, take the money. As you get older, the money will become your sex appeal. - Katherine Hepburn

The worst moment for the atheist is when he feels thankful and has no one to thank. - Dante Gabriel Rossetti

Success is liking yourself, liking what you do, and liking how you do it. - Maya Angelou

The best way to cheer yourself up is to cheer somebody else up. - Mark Twain

It's easy to identify people who can't count to ten. They're in front of you in the supermarket express lane. - M. Grundler

Death is psychologically as important as birth. Shrinking away from it is something unhealthy and abnormal which robs the second half of life of its purpose. - Carl Jung

We hold these truths to be self-evident: that all men are created equal; that they are endowed by their Creator with certain unalienable rights; that among these are life, liberty, and the pursuit of happiness. - Thomas Jefferson

Never explain--your friends do not need it and your enemies will not believe you anyway. - Elbert Hubbard

Freedom means the opportunity to be what we never thought we would be. - Daniel J. Boorstin

Time is money. - Benjamin Franklin

Life is a compromise of what your ego wants to do, what experience tells you to do, and what your nerves let you do.

Dancing is a perpendicular expression of a horizontal desire. - George Bernard Shaw

Half a truth is often a great lie. - Benjamin Franklin

The odds of not meeting in this life are so great that every meeting is like a miracle. It's a wonder that we don't make love to every single person we meet. - Yoko Ono

A man will fight harder for his interests than for his rights. - Napoleon Bonaparte

A man doesn't want a child - he is a dead beat dad. A woman doesn't want a child - she is pro-choice.

The man who regards life as meaningless is not merely unfortunate, but almost disqualified for life. - Albert Einstein

The nationalist not only does not disapprove of atrocities committed by his own side, but he has a remarkable capacity for not even hearing about them. - George Orwell

I think, at a child's birth, if a mother could ask a fairy godmother to endow it with the most useful gift, that gift should be curiosity. - Eleanor Roosevelt

No problem is so formidable that you can't walk away from it. - Charles Schulz

I keep my good health by having a very bad temper, kept under good control. - Theodore Roosevelt

The world is moving so fast these days that the man who says it can't be done is generally interrupted by someone doing it. - Elbert Hubbard

To photograph truthfully and effectively is to see beneath the surfaces and record the qualities of nature and humanity which live or are latent in all things. - Ansel Adams

I have friends in overalls whose friendship I would not swap for the favor of the kings of the world. - Thomas Edison

When I took office, only high energy physicists had ever heard of what is called the Worldwide Web....now even my cat has its own page. - Bill Clinton

Many people lose their tempers merely from seeing you keep yours. - Frank Moore Colby

I saw this in a movie about a bus that had to SPEED around a city, keeping its SPEED over fifty, and if its SPEED dropped, it would explode! I think it was called, 'The Bus That Couldn't Slow Down.' - Homer Simpson

To ridicule philosophy is really to philosophize. - Blaise Pascal

Faith is the art of holding on to things your reason once accepted, despite your changing moods. - C.S. Lewis

Every step we take towards making the State our Caretaker of our lives, by that much we move toward making the State our Master. - Dwight Eisenhower

Life cannot be prolonged, therefore make use of it as best as you can for your betterment and for the good of others.

―――――――――〜―――――――

Forgive, O Lord, my little jokes on Thee, and I'll forgive Thy great big joke on me. - Robert Frost

―――――――――〜―――――――

The man you most admire is the type of man you ought to be.

―――――――――〜―――――――

Indeed, man wishes to be happy even when he so lives as to make happiness impossible. - Saint Augustine

―――――――――〜―――――――

I hate to advocate drugs, alcohol, violence, or insanity to anyone, but they've always worked for me. - Hunter S. Thompson

It is strangely absurd to suppose that a million of human beings, collected together, are not under the same moral laws which bind each of them separately. - Thomas Jefferson

The most depraved type of being is that without purpose. - Ayn Rand

Help your brother to climb the hill and you will find yourself nearer to the top.

A great fortune in the hands of a fool is a great misfortune.

To live is the rarest thing in the world. Most people exist, that is all. - Oscar Wilde

All theoretical chemistry is really physics; and all theoretical chemists know it. - Richard P. Feynman

Try to exclude the possibility of suffering which the order of nature and the existence of free-wills involve, and you find that you have excluded life itself. - C.S. Lewis

Wisdom begins at the end. - Daniel Webster

Nature thrives on patience; man on impatience. - Paul Boese

I object to violence because when it appears to do good, the good is only temporary; the evil it does is permanent. - Mahatma Gandhi

When men are full of envy they disparage
everything, whether it be good or bad. - Tacitus

If you cannot lift the load off another's back, do not
walk away. Try to lighten it. - Frank Tyger

Despair is the conclusion of fools. - Benjamin Disraeli

Desire, definiteness, determination and daring are
achievement in any great endeavor.

No government ever voluntarily reduces itself in
size. - Ronald Reagan

If you don't have a competitive advantage, don't
compete - Jack Welch

People only see what they are prepared to see. - Ralph Waldo Emerson

I just want to do God's will. - Martin Luther King Jr.

There are a lot of lies going around...and half of them are true. - Winston Churchill

You are not special. You are not a beautiful or unique snowflake. You are the same decaying organic matter as everything else. - Chuck Palahniuk

The higher your structure is to be, the deeper must be its foundation. - Saint Augustine

The secret of business is to know something that nobody else knows. - Aristotle Onassis

Wisdom is knowing what to do next, skill is knowing how to do it, and virtue is doing it.

The secret to humor is surprise. - Aristotle

Why should we take advice on sex from the pope? If he knows anything about it, he shouldn't! - George Bernard Shaw

Politics is the art of looking for trouble, finding it everywhere, diagnosing it incorrectly, and applying the wrong remedies. - Groucho Marx

God whispers to us in our pleasures, speaks in our conscience, but shouts in our pains: it is His megaphone to rouse a deaf world. - C.S. Lewis

Wit is educated insolence. - Aristotle

Live daringly, boldly, fearlessly. Taste the relish to be found in competition in having put forth the best within you. - Henry J. Kaiser

Friendship may, and often does, grow into love, but love never subsides into friendship. - Lord Byron

If life was fair, Elvis would be alive and all the impersonators would be dead. - Johnny Carson

A man is not finished when he is defeated. He is finished when he quits. – Richard Nixon

Prediction is very difficult, especially about the future. - Niels Bohr

How I wish that somewhere there existed an island for those who are wise and of goodwill! In such a place even I would be an ardent patriot. - Albert Einstein

For centuries, theologians have been explaining the unknowable in terms of the-not-worth-knowing. - Henry Mencken

We must accept finite disappointment, but never lose infinite hope. - Martin Luther King Jr.

He who rejects change is the architect of decay. The only human institution which rejects progress is the cemetery. - Harold Wilson

---

Children are educated by what the grown-up is and not by his talk. - Carl Jung

---

Capital isn't scarce; vision is - Sam Walton

The reason we hold truth in such respect is because we have so little opportunity to get familiar with it. - Mark Twain

---

Sometimes when you innovate, you make mistakes. It is best to admit them quickly, and get on with improving your other innovations. - Steve Jobs

A country cannot subsist well without liberty, nor liberty without virtue. - Daniel Webster

———————⁓———————

Bad men cannot make good citizens. A vitiated state of morals, a corrupted public conscience are incompatible with freedom. - Patrick Henry

———————⁓———————

Of all noises, I think music is the least disagreeable. - Samuel Johnson

———————⁓———————

Americans are so enamored of equality; they would rather be equal in slavery than unequal in freedom. - Alexis de Tocqueville

———————⁓———————

Let your eyes look at kindness, your tongue speak with mildness and your hands touch with softness.

Man will ultimately be governed by God or by tyrants. - Benjamin Franklin

---

No evil can happen to a good man, either in life or after death. - Plato

---

We are going to have peace even if we have to fight for it. - Dwight Eisenhower

---

I've never learned anything while I was talking. - Larry King

---

The easiest way to live happily is to live honestly.

Are you bored with life? Then throw yourself into some work you believe in with all your heart, live for it, die for it, and you will find happiness that you had thought could never be yours. - Dale Carnegie

We are healed from suffering only by experiencing it to the full. - Marcel Proust

It's not about finding the right man; it's about being the right woman. - Debby Jones

The invisible and the non-existent look very much alike. - Delos McKown

Knowledge rests not upon truth alone, but upon error also. - Carl Jung

I guess the only way to stop divorce is to stop marriage. - Will Rogers

---

Never be a prisoner of your past. Become the architect of your future, building every day

---

Out of Debt, Out of Danger. - Proverb

Which painting in the National Gallery would I save if there was a fire? The one nearest the door of course. - George Bernard Shaw

---

There never was a good war or a bad peace. - Benjamin Franklin

---

The intellect is not a serious thing, and never has been. It is an instrument on which one plays, that is all. - Oscar Wilde

You don't need to be 'straight' to fight and die for your country. You just need to shoot straight. - Barry Goldwater

There are two types of education. One should teach us how to make a living, and the other how to live. - John Adams

If you would persuade, you must appeal to interest rather than intellect. - Benjamin Franklin

Take the diplomacy out of war and the thing would fall flat in a week. - Will Rogers

Inside every working anarchy, there's an Old Boy Network. - Mitchell Kapor

I'm totally at home on the stage. That's where I live. That's where I was born. That's where I'm safe. - Michael Jackson

Sin lies only in hurting other people unnecessarily. All other 'sins' are invented nonsense. - Robert Heinlein

If I ran a school, I'd give the average grade to the ones who gave me all the right answers, for being good parrots. I'd give the top grades to those who made a lot of mistakes and told me about them, and then told me what they learned from them. - Buckminster Fuller

Troubles are often the tools by which God fashions us for better things.

That enlightened one who is brave alike in pleasure and pain, he becomes eligible for immortality.

This truth should be kept constantly in mind by every free people desiring to preserve the sanity and poise indispensable to the permanent success of self-government. - Theodore Roosevelt

I know not what course others make take, but as for me: give me Liberty, or give me death. - Patrick Henry

If you don't say anything, you won't be called on to repeat it. - Calvin Coolidge

You don't take a photograph, you make it. - Ansel Adams

The permanent temptation of life is to confuse dreams with reality. The permanent defeat of life comes when dreams are surrendered to reality. - James Michener

It's a damn poor mind that can only think of one way to spell a word. - Andrew Jackson

The path to greatness is along with others. - Baltasar Gracian

The greatest lesson in life is to know that even fools are right sometimes. - Winston Churchill

The leader who exercises power with honor will work from the inside out, starting with himself. - Blaine Lee

---

If you can't accept losing, you can't win. - Vince Lombardi

Don't confuse fame with success. Madonna is one; Helen Keller is the other. - Erna Bombeck

---

Blessed are the forgetful: for they get the better even of their blunders. - Friedrich Nietzsche

---

Most of the change we think we see in life is due to truths being in and out of favor. - Robert Frost

---

To be what we are, and to become what we are capable of becoming, is the only end of life. - Robert Louis Stevenson

Providence has given us hope and sleep as a compensation for the many care of life - Voltaire

I think that a hat which has a little cannon that fires and then goes back inside the hat is at least a decade away. - Jack Handey

Golf is a game whose aim is to hit a very small ball into an even smaller hole, with weapons singularly ill-designed for the purpose. - Winston Churchill

The best index to a person's character is (a) how he treats people who can't do him any good, and (b) how he treats people who can't fight back. - Abigail Van Buren

When ideas fail, words come in very handy. - Johann Wolfgang von Goethe

It is a general popular error to suppose the loudest complainers for the public to be the most anxious for its welfare. - Edmund Burke

It is difficult, but not impossible, to conduct strictly honest business. - Mahatma Gandhi

Old age comes on suddenly, and not gradually as is thought. - Emily Dickinson

Never compromise your values and beliefs, even if it means risking ridicule and rejection. Be true to yourself.

―――――――――~――――――

If we desire to avoid insult, we must be able to repel it; if we desire to secure peace, one of the most powerful instruments of our rising prosperity, it must be known, that we are at all times ready for War. - George Washington

―――――――――~――――――

Looking back, I have this to regret, that too often when I loved, I did not say so. - David Grayson

―――――――――~――――――

It takes a great deal of bravery to stand up to your enemies, but a great deal more to stand up to your friends – Dumbledore, Harry Potter

―――――――――~――――――

Too much of a good thing can be wonderful. - Mae West

Never tell the truth to people who are not worthy of it. - Mark Twain

I tremble for my country when I reflect that God is just, that His justice cannot sleep forever. - Thomas Jefferson

Don't use words too big for the subject. Don't say 'infinitely' when you mean 'very'; otherwise you'll have no word left when you want to talk about something really infinite. - C.S. Lewis

Wherever any precept of traditional morality is simply challenged to produce its credentials, as though the burden of proof lay on it, we have taken the wrong position. - C.S. Lewis

---

It is astonishing what an effort it seems to be for many people to put their brains definitely and systematically to work. - Thomas Edison

---

Love is a verb.

Arbitrary power is most easily established on the ruins of liberty abused to licentiousness. - George Washington

---

Try, try, try, and keep on trying is the rule that must be followed to become an expert in anything. - W. Clement Stone

No change of circumstances can repair a defect of character. - Ralph Waldo Emerson

The most important quality in a leader is that of being acknowledged as such. All leaders whose fitness is questioned are clearly lacking in force. - Andre Maurois

Mothers all want their sons to grow up to be president, but they don't want them to become politicians in the process. - John F. Kennedy

The point of philosophy is to start with something so simple as not to seem worth stating and to end with something so paradoxical that no one will believe it. - Bertrand Russell

I would like to take you seriously, but to do so would affront your intelligence. - William F. Buckley

---

Immature love says: 'I love you because I need you.' Mature love says: 'I need you because I love you.' - Erich Fromm

---

Faith changes hope into reality. - Kenneth E Hagin

The NBA is never just a business. It's always business. It's always personal. All good businesses are personal. The best businesses are very personal - Mark Cuban

---

A joyful heart is like the sunshine of God's love, the hope of eternal happiness. - Mother Teresa

That men do not learn very much from the lessons of history is the most important of all the lessons of history. - Aldous Huxley

———————⌇———————

A poem begins as a lump in the throat, a sense of wrong, a homesickness, a lovesickness. - Robert Frost

———————⌇———————

Tragedy is when I cut my finger. Comedy is when you walk into an open sewer and die. - Mel Brooks

———————⌇———————

It is an animal instinct to do harm to other creatures - Swami Chinmayananda

———————⌇———————

To be wise and love exceeds man's might. - William Shakespeare

———————⌇———————

Success didn't spoil me, I've always been insufferable. - Fran Lebowitz

———————～———————

Speaking the Truth in times of universal deceit is a revolutionary act. - George Orwell

———————～———————

Good judgment comes from experience. Experience comes from bad judgment. - Jim Horning

———————～———————

Why should people go out and pay money to see bad films when they can stay at home and see bad television for nothing? - Samuel Goldwyn

———————～———————

The ear is the only true writer and the only true reader. - Robert Frost

———————～———————

When the human race has once acquired a superstition nothing short of death is ever likely to remove it. - Mark Twain

Progress is impossible without change, and those who cannot change their minds cannot change anything. - George Bernard Shaw

Neither a man nor a crowd nor a nation can be trusted to act humanely or to think sanely under the influence of a great fear. - Bertrand Russell

A good many young writers make the mistake of enclosing a stamped, self-addressed envelope, big enough for the manuscript to come back in. This is too much of a temptation to the editor. - Ring Lardner

Freedom is the right to question and change the established way of doing things. It is the continuous revolution of the marketplace. It is the understanding that allows us to recognize shortcomings and seek solutions. - Ronald Reagan

I love deadlines. I especially like the whooshing sound they make as they go flying by. - Douglas Adams

Freedom of the press is limited to those who own one. - Henry Mencken

Friends, if we be honest with ourselves, we shall be honest with each other. - George MacDonald

The weakness of men is the facade of strength; the strength of women is the facade of weakness. - Lawrence Diggs

Dualism is a truncated metaphysic. - C.S. Lewis

Wisdom and good judgment life together, for wisdom knows where to discover knowledge and understanding.

The riddles of God are more satisfying than the solutions of man. - GK Chesterton

The Vietnam War required us to emphasize the national interest rather than abstract principles. - Henry Kissinger

A man never tells you anything until you contradict him. - George Bernard Shaw

Have you ever heard people say 'don't sweat the details'? Well, they're wrong: sweat the details. They have a name for people who sweat the details: millionaires. - Jerry Bowyer

When I am working on a problem I never think about beauty. I only think about how to solve the problem. But when I have finished, if the solution is not beautiful, I know it is wrong. - Buckminster Fuller

On my way here I passed a local cinema and it turned out you were expecting me after all, for the billboards read: The Mummy Returns. - Margaret Thatcher

Our destiny is bound up with the destiny of every other American. - Bill Clinton

War is an instrument entirely inefficient toward redressing wrong; and multiplies, instead of indemnifying losses. - Thomas Jefferson

No virtuous act is quite as virtuous from the standpoint of our friend or foe, as from our own. Therefore, we are saved by the final form of love which is forgiveness. - Reinhold Niebuhr

Truth is so rare that it is delightful to tell it. - Emily Dickinson

Big pay and little responsibility are circumstances seldom found together - Napoleon Hill

Reason and judgment are the qualities of a leader. - Tacitus

Identifying ourselves with the body is putting the cart before the horse and this is why we stumble in life.

Anger will never disappear so long as thoughts of resentment are cherished in the mind. Anger will disappear just as soon as thoughts of resentment are forgotten. - Siddhartha Buddha

---

Everyone who is incapable of learning has taken to teaching. - Oscar Wilde

You can fool some of the people all of the time, and all of the people some of the time. But you cannot fool all of the people all of the time. - Abraham Lincoln

The poets have been mysteriously silent on the subject of cheese. - GK Chesterton

God offers to every mind its choice between truth and repose. Take which you please - you can never have both. - Ralph Waldo Emerson

Management is nothing more than motivating other people. - Le Iacocca

Any man's death diminishes me, because I am involved in Mankind; and therefore never send to know for whom the bell tolls; it tolls for thee. - John Donne

A virtuous wife is a man's best treasure.

This country will not be a good place for any of us to live in unless we make it a good place for all of us to live in. - Theodore Roosevelt

Don't you wish you had a job like mine? All you have to do is think up a certain number of words! Plus, you can repeat words! And they don't even have to be true! - Dave Barry

George Washington, as a boy, was ignorant of the commonest accomplishments of youth. He could not even lie. - Mark Twain

To write a good love letter, you ought to begin without knowing what you mean to say and to finish without knowing what you have written. - Jean-Jacques Rousseau

Peace you crave for is ever within you. If you seek it from without, you will never have it anywhere - Swami Ramdas

Feel no sadness because of evil thoughts: it only strengthens them. - Nachman of Bratslav

Freedom is not an ideal, it is not even a protection, if it means nothing more than freedom to stagnate, to live without dreams, to have no greater aim than a second car and another television set. - Adlai Stevenson

My theology, briefly, is that the universe was dictated but not signed. - Christopher Morley

Many interviewers when they come to talk to me, think they're being progressive by not mentioning in their stories any longer that I'm black. I tell them, 'Don't stop now. If I shot somebody you'd mention it.' - Colin Powell

I'm so fast that, last night, I turned off the light switch in my hotel room and was in bed before the room was dark. - Muhammad Ali

We should not judge a man's merit by his good qualities but by the use he can make of them.

History does not long entrust the care of freedom to the weak or the timid. - Dwight Eisenhower

The beauty of religious mania is that it has the power to explain everything. Once God (or Satan) is accepted as the first cause of everything which happens in the mortal world, nothing is left to chance... logic can be happily tossed out the window. - Stephen King

Cast your cares on God; that anchor holds. - Frank Moore Colby

I have found the paradox that if I love until it hurts, then there is no hurt, but only more love. - Mother Teresa

Marriage is not a ritual or an end. It is a long, intricate, intimate dance together and nothing matters more than your own sense of balance and your choice of partner. - Amy Bloom

It is a common observation here that our cause is the cause of all mankind, and that we are fighting for their liberty in defending our own. - Benjamin Franklin

Labor to keep alive in your breast that little spark of celestial fire called conscience. - George Washington

The only secure knowledge is that I exist. - Rene Descartes

War with evil; but show no spirit of malignity toward the man who may be responsible for the evil. Put it out of his power to do wrong. - Theodore Roosevelt

---

The federal government has taken too much tax money from the people, too much authority from the states, and too much liberty with the Constitution. - Ronald Reagan

---

Faith may be defined briefly as an illogical belief in the occurrence of the improbable. - Henry Mencken

---

If a nation expects to be ignorant and free, in a state of civilization, it expects what never was and never will be. - Thomas Jefferson

He that falls in love with himself will have no rivals. - Benjamin Franklin

Any mental activity is easy if it need not take reality into account. - Marcel Proust

War is an art and as such is not susceptible of explanation by fixed formula. - George Patton

The flames kindled on the Fourth of July, 1776, have spread over too much of the globe to be extinguished by the feeble engines of despotism; on the contrary, they will consume these engines and all who work them. - Thomas Jefferson

Money doesn't talk, it swears. - Bob Dylan

Love is needing to be loved. - John Lennon

Only one man in a thousand is a leader of men. The other 999 follow women. - Groucho Marx

The most incomprehensible thing about the world is that it is at all comprehensible. - Albert Einstein

There are no such things as limits to growth, because there are no limits on the human capacity for intelligence, imagination and wonder. - Ronald Reagan

We've had bad luck with our kids - they've all grown up. - Christopher Morley

Life does not cease to be funny when people die any more than it ceases to be serious when people laugh. - George Bernard Shaw

Always be on time. Do as little talking as humanly possible. Remember to lean back in the parade so everybody can see the president. Be sure not to get too fat, because you'll have to sit three in the back. - Eleanor Roosevelt

Moderation is a virtue only in those who are thought to have an alternative. - Henry Kissinger

Our liberty depends on the freedom of the press, and that cannot be limited without being lost. - Thomas Jefferson

Real freedom is having nothing. I was freer when I didn't have a cent. - Mike Tyson

There is no joy in life like the joy of sharing. - Billy Graham

The value of an idea lies in the using of it. - Thomas Edison

There are perhaps no days of our childhood we lived so fully as those we spent with a favorite book. - Marcel Proust

My observation is that whenever one person is found adequate to the discharge of a duty. It is worse executed by two persons, and scarcely done at all if three or more are employed therein. - George Washington

There is no finer investment for any community than putting milk into babies. - Winston Churchill

Where all think alike, no one thinks very much. - Walter Lippman

The only thing we have to fear is fear itself - nameless, unreasoning, unjustified terror which paralyzes needed efforts to convert retreat into advance. - Franklin D. Roosevelt

Have you ever observed that we pay much more attention to a wise passage when it is quoted than when we read it in the original author? - Philip Hamerton

Nature does nothing uselessly. - Aristotle

One thing only I know, and that is that I know nothing. - Socrates

The IQ and the life expectancy of the average American recently passed each other going in the opposite direction. - George Carlin

You can make more friends in two months by becoming interested in other people than you can in two years by trying to get other people interested in you. - Dale Carnegie

The prosperity of a country can be seen simply in how it treats its old people. - Nachman of Bratslav

---

Slang is the language which takes off its coat, spits on its hands - and goes to work. - Carl Sandburg

---

All but the hard hearted man must be torn with pity for this pathetic dilemma of the rich man, who has to keep the poor man just stout enough to do the work and just thin enough to have to do it. - GK Chesterton

---

When we give undue respect to some people, sometimes, we do not get even due respect.

He that would live in peace and at ease must not speak all he knows or all he sees. - Benjamin Franklin

The significant problems we face cannot be solved at the same level of thinking we were at when we created them. - Albert Einstein

I think computer viruses should count as life. I think it says something about human nature that the only form of life we have created so far is purely destructive. We've created life in our own image. - Stephen Hawking

Scientists make a guess and call it a hypothesis. 'Guess' is too short a word for a professor. - William Jennings Bryan

If he persists in saying to me what he likes, he shall hear what he does not like - Terence

If you are in search of the greatest treasure, don't look outside, look within, seek3 that.

One of the greatest things in life is not so much where we are, but in what direction we are moving.

To see what is in front of one's nose needs a constant struggle. - George Orwell

Success is going from failure to failure without losing enthusiasm. - Winston Churchill

The mode by which the inevitable comes to pass is effort. - Oliver Wendell Holmes

If you would be known, and not know, vegetate in a village; If you would know, and not be known, live in a city. - Charles Caleb Colton

I love the man that can smile in trouble that can gather strength from distress, and grow brave by reflection. - Thomas Paine

The first duty of love is to listen. - Paul Tillich

Art can teach without at all ceasing to be art. - C.S. Lewis

He who is of calm and happy nature will hardly feel the pressure of age, but to him who is of an opposite disposition youth and age are equally a burden. - Plato

If you are going to win any battle, you have to do one thing. You have to make the mind run the body. Never let the body tell the mind what to do... the body is never tired if the mind is not tired. - George Patton

Every man over forty is a scoundrel. - George Bernard Shaw

The thing we all have to understand to put these last two years in focus, is that liberals in this country care more about whether European leaders like us than they do about whether terrorists are killing us. - Rush Limbaugh

Anyone who has never made a mistake has never tried anything new. - Albert Einstein

Freedom is not a gift bestowed upon us by other men, but a right that belongs to us by the laws of God and nature. - Benjamin Franklin

Most football teams are temperamental. That's 90% temper and 10% mental. - Doug Plank

If you keep doing what you've always done, you'll always get what you've always gotten. - John C Maxwell

I can picture in my mind a world without war, a world without hate. And I can picture us attacking that world, because they'd never expect it. - Jack Handey

The statistics on sanity are that one out of every four Americans are suffering from some form of mental illness. Think of your three best friends. If they're okay, then it's you. - Rita Mae Brown

———————⌇———————

I don't embrace trouble; that's as bad as treating it as an enemy. But I do say meet it as a friend, for you'll see a lot of it and had better be on speaking terms with it. - Oliver Wendell Holmes

———————⌇———————

You are educated. Your certification is in your degree. You may think of it as the ticket to the good life. Let me ask you to think of an alternative. Think of it as your ticket to change the world. - Tom Brokaw

———————⌇———————

Become a POSSIBILITARIAN. No matter how dark things seem to be or actually are, raise your sights and see possibilities- always see them, for they're always there. - Norman Vincent Peale

There is no strength in unbelief. Even the unbelief of what is false is no source of might. It is the truth shining from behind that gives the strength to disbelieve. - George MacDonald

Before God we are all equally wise and equally foolish. - Albert Einstein

There is no greater hell than to be a prisoner of fear. - Ben Jonson

The world is a fine place, and worth fighting for. - Ernest Hemingway

I didn't come to Washington to be loved and I haven't been disappointed. - Philip L. Gramm

Cowards die many times before their deaths. The valiant never taste of death but once. - William Shakespeare

What is happiness? The feeling that power is growing, that resistance is overcome. - Friedrich Nietzsche

I wanted to change the world. But I have found that the only thing one can be sure of changing is oneself. - Aldous Huxley

I planted some bird seed. A bird came up. Now I don't know what to feed it. - Steven Wright

Critics who treat 'adult' as a term of approval, instead of as a merely descriptive term, cannot be adult themselves. - C.S. Lewis

You won't get anything unless you have the vision to imagine it. - John Lennon

———————～———————

You have the power to make happiness a way of life, instead of an occasional experience.

———————～———————

I do not feel obliged to believe that the same God who has endowed us with sense, reason, and intellect has intended us to forgo their use. - Galileo Galilei

———————～———————

Black holes are where God divided by zero. - Steven Wright

———————～———————

If you start to think about your physical or moral condition, you usually find that you are sick. - Johann Wolfgang von Goethe

Associate yourself with men of good quality if you esteem your own reputation; for 'tis better to be alone than in bad company. - George Washington

---

Of course the meek will inherit the earth, what, did you think they'd take it by force?

Find out how much God has given you and from it take what you need; the remainder is needed by others. - Saint Augustine

---

Wealth is the parent of luxury and indolence, and poverty of meanness and viciousness, and both of discontent. - Plato

---

Who does not thank for little will not thank for much.

Silence is one of the hardest arguments to refute. - Josh Billings

In all chaos there is a cosmos, in all disorder a secret order. - Carl Jung

The country shall be independent, and we will be satisfied with nothing short of it. - Samuel Adams

You don't have to stay up nights to succeed; you have to stay awake days.

Don't handicap your children by making their lives easy. - Robert A. Heinlein

The highest form of ignorance is when you reject something you don't know anything about. - Wayne Dyer

My philosophy is that not only are you responsible for your life, but doing the best at this moment puts you in the best place for the next moment. - Oprah Winfrey

This most beautiful system [The Universe] could only proceed from the dominion of an intelligent and powerful Being. - Isaac Newton

Humanity is acquiring all the right technology for all the wrong reasons. - Buckminster Fuller

Just as a candle cannot burn without fire, men cannot live without a spiritual life. - Siddhartha Buddha

What difference does it make to the dead, the orphans and the homeless whether the mad destruction is brought under the name of totalitarianism or the holy name of liberty and democracy? - Mahatma Gandhi

The baby rises to its feet, takes a step, is overcome with triumph and joy - and falls flat on its face. It is a pattern for all that is to come! But learn from the bewildered baby. Lurch to your feet again. You'll make the sofa in the end. - Pam Brown

There is one thing about being President; no one can tell you when to sit down. - Dwight Eisenhower

Education is like a double-edged sword. It may be turned to dangerous uses if it is not properly handled. - Wu Ting-Fang

Whoso loves believes the impossible. - Elizabeth Barrett Browning

I am a thing that thinks, that is to say, a thing that doubts, affirms, denies, understands a few things, is ignorant of many things, wills, refrains from willing, and also imagines and senses. - Rene Descartes

What we're really talking about is a wonderful day set aside on the fourth Thursday of November when no one diets. I mean, why else would they call it Thanksgiving? - Erna Bombeck

It is an unfortunate fact that we can secure peace only by preparing for war. - John F. Kennedy

Heav'n hath no rage like love to hatred turn'd, Nor Hell a fury, like a woman scorn'd. - William Congreve

The first maxim of the right path is to tell the truth, to think the truth and act the truth - Mahatma Gandhi

It was the experience of mystery -- even if mixed with fear -- that engendered religion. - Albert Einstein

I'm astounded by people who want to 'know' the universe when it's hard enough to find your way around Chinatown. - Woody Allen

In America the majority raises formidable barriers around the liberty of opinion; within these barriers an author may write what he pleases, but woe to him if he goes beyond them. - Alexis de Tocqueville

The eyes of the world are upon you. The hopes and prayers of liberty-loving people everywhere march with you. - Dwight Eisenhower

What do I know about sex? I'm a married man. - Tom Clancy

Regarding the debate about faith and works: It's like asking which blade in a pair of scissors is most important. - C.S. Lewis

I destroy my enemies when I make them my friends. - Abraham Lincoln

Have children while your parents are still young enough to take care of them. - Rita Rudner

---

Before everything else, getting ready is the secret of success. - Henry Ford

---

Bad men live that they may eat and drink, whereas good men eat and drink that they may live. - Socrates

---

You are stronger than you know. – Lori Osterman

One cannot do right in one area of life while he is occupied in doing wrong in another. Life is one indivisible whole.

My therapist told me the way to achieve true inner peace is to finish what I start. So far today, I have finished 2 bags of M&M's and a chocolate cake. I feel better already. - Dave Barry

The noblest search is the search for excellence - Lyndon B. Johnson

I've noticed that everybody that is for abortion has already been born. - Ronald Reagan

The American temptation is to believe that foreign policy is a subdivision of psychiatry. - Henry Kissinger

Remember not only to say the right thing in the right place, but far more difficult still, to leave unsaid the wrong thing at the tempting moment. - Benjamin Franklin

Good intentions will always be pleaded for every assumption of authority. It is hardly too strong to say that the Constitution was made to guard the people against the dangers of good intentions. - Daniel Webster

To wage a war for a purely moral reason is as absurd as to ravish a woman for a purely moral reason. - Henry Mencken

Life is no brief candle to me. It is a sort of splendid torch which I have got a hold of for the moment, and I want to make it burn as brightly as possible before handing it onto future generations. - George Bernard Shaw

He loves but little who can say and count in words how much he loves. - Dante Alighieri

---

In politics stupidity is not a handicap. - Napoleon Bonaparte

---

I am ready to meet my Maker. Whether my Maker is prepared for the great ordeal of meeting me is another matter. - Winston Churchill

---

The greatest monarch on the proudest throne is obliged to sit upon his own arse. - Benjamin Franklin

---

I buy when other people are selling. - J. Paul Getty

From such beginnings of governments, what could be expected, but a continual system of war and extortion? - Thomas Paine

The worst thing that could happen to anybody, would be to not be used for anything by anybody. - Kurt Vonnegut

We are made wise not by the recollection of our past, but by the responsibility for our future. - George Bernard Shaw

Classical music gradually lost popularity because it is too complicated: you need twenty-five or thirty skilled musicians just to hum it properly. So people began to develop regular music. - Dave Barry

There is nothing holier in this life of ours than the first consciousness of love.

I must have a prodigious quantity of mind; it takes me as much as a week sometimes to make it up. - Mark Twain

---

Democracy is based upon the conviction that there are extraordinary possibilities in ordinary people.

To show resentment at a reproach is to acknowledge that one may have deserved it. - Tacitus

---

Age does not protect you from love, but love to some extent protects you from age. - Jeanne Moreau

I would rather have peace in the world than be President. - Harry Truman

The older I grow the more I distrust the familiar doctrine that age brings wisdom. - Henry Mencken

Anyone can get old; all you have to do is live long enough. - Groucho Marx

If nothing every went wrong in your life, you would never have a chance to grow stronger.

Cheerfulness keeps up the spirit of the one who possesses it, and brings a smile to the lips of others.

Men don't care what is on TV. They only care what else is on TV. – Jerry Seinfeld

It seemed the world was divided into good and bad people. The good ones slept better, while the bad ones seemed to enjoy the waking hours much more. - Woody Allen

You gain strength, experience and confidence by every experience where you really stop to look fear in the face. You must do the thing you cannot do. - Eleanor Roosevelt

Democracy is a process by which people are free to choose the man who will get the blame. - Laurence Peter

Physical bravery is an animal instinct; moral bravery is a much higher and truer courage - Wendell Phillips

———————～———————

People who say you're just as old as you feel are all wrong, fortunately. - Russell Baker

———————～———————

The artist is a receptacle for emotions that come from all over the place: from the sky, from the earth, from a scrap of paper, from a passing shape. - Pablo Picasso

———————～———————

I came, I saw, I conquered. - Julius Caesar

———————～———————

Arbitration is justice blended with charity. - Nachman of Bratslav

The difference between Los Angeles and yogurt is that yogurt comes with less fruit. - Rush Limbaugh

Scientists tell us that the fastest animal on earth, with a top speed of 120 ft./sec, is a cow that has been dropped out of a helicopter. - Dave Barry

A cynic is a man who knows the price of everything and the value of nothing. - Oscar Wilde

Everything has its beauty, but not everyone sees it. - Confucius

It does not mean that the enemy is to be allowed to escape. The object is to make him believe that there is a road to safety, and thus prevent his fighting with the courage of despair. After that, you may crush him. - Sun Tzu

If you want to make peace, you don't talk to your friends. You talk to your enemies. - Moshe Dayan

Politics is such a torment that I advise everyone I love not to mix with it. - Thomas Jefferson

You got to be very careful if you don't know where you're going, because you might not get there. - Yogi Berra

I have never in my life learned anything from any man who agreed with me. - Dudley Malone

Guard with jealous attention the public liberty. Suspect everyone who approaches that jewel. - Patrick Henry

My one regret in life is that I am not someone else. - Woody Allen

The best reason to start an organization is to make meaning; to create a product or service to make the world a better place - Guy Kawasaki

Never interrupt me when I'm trying to interrupt you. - Winston Churchill

If man could have half his wishes, he would double his troubles - Benjamin Franklin

On life's journey faith is nourishment, virtuous deeds are a shelter, wisdom is the light by day and right mindfulness is the protection by night. If a man lives a pure life, nothing can destroy him. - Siddhartha Buddha

Kids, just because I don't care doesn't mean I'm not listening. - Homer Simpson

The greatest test of courage on earth is to bear defeat without losing heart – Robert Ingersoll

If there is any principle of the Constitution that more imperatively calls for attachment than any other it is the principle of free thought, not free thought for those who agree with us but freedom for the thought that we hate. - Oliver Wendell Holmes

He is a great man who uses earthenware dishes as if they were silver, but he is equally great who uses silver as if they were earthenware.

As the circle of light increases, so does the circumference of darkness around it. - Albert Einstein

I have discovered photography. Now I can kill myself. I have nothing else to learn. - Pablo Picasso

I would not know how I am supposed to feel about many stories if not for the fact that the TV news personalities make sad faces for sad stories and happy faces for happy stories. - Dave Barry

You will only go as far as you think you can go.

Those who expect to reap the blessings of freedom must, like men, undergo the fatigue of supporting it. - Thomas Paine

Famous remarks are very seldom quoted correctly. - Simeon Strunsky

The soul of one who loves God always swims in joy and always is in a mood for singing.

There is a great deal of difference between an eager man who wants to read a book and the tired man who wants a book to read. - GK Chesterton

To see what is right and yet shrink from doing it is for want of courage.

But when I got to be 21, I was astonished at how much the old man had learned in seven years. - Mark Twain

If a woman has to choose between catching a fly ball and saving an infant's life, she will choose to save the infant's life without even considering if there are men on base. - Dave Barry

Great leaders are almost always great simplifiers, who can cut through argument, debate, and doubt to offer a solution everybody can understand. - Colin Powell

Without meditation where is peace, without peace where is happiness?

This film cost $31 million. With that kind of money I could have invaded some country. - Clint Eastwood

Let everyone that you meet be happier for having met you, for having spoken to you. This you can do by spreading joy.

Human beings are the only creatures that allow their children to come back home. - Bill Cosby

My life is my message. - Mahatma Gandhi

No easy problem ever comes to the President of the United States. If they are easy to solve, somebody else has solved them. - John F. Kennedy

We've all heard that a million monkeys banging on a million typewriters will eventually reproduce the entire works of Shakespeare. Now, thanks to the Internet, we know this is not true. - Robert Wilensky

Duties are not performed for duty's sake, but because their neglect would make the man uncomfortable. A man performs but one duty - the duty of contenting his spirit, the duty of making himself agreeable to himself. - Mark Twain

---

Love is space and time measured by the heart. - Marcel Proust

---

Millions saw the apple fall, but Newton was the one who asked why. - Bernard Baruch

---

In science one tries to tell people, in such a way as to be understood by everyone, something that no one ever knew before. But in poetry, it's the exact opposite. - Paul Dirac

Pray as though everything depended on God. Work as though everything depended on you. - Saint Augustine

The courage we desire and prize, is not the courage to die decently but to live manfully - Carlyle

He who loves 50 people has 50 woes; he who loves no one has no woes. - Siddhartha Buddha

Those who trust to chance must abide by the results of chance. - Calvin Coolidge

The devil made me do it the first time, and after that I did it on my own. - Robert Fulghum

The World is a book, and those who do not travel read only a page. - Saint Augustine

———～———

There are men in all ages who mean to govern well, but they mean to govern. They promise to be good masters, but they mean to be masters. - Daniel Webster

———～———

A myth is a religion in which no one any longer believes. - James Feibleman

———～———

It is not what you look at, but what you see. - Henry Thoreau

———～———

All art is quite useless. - Oscar Wilde

———～———

An inconvenience is only an adventure wrongly considered; an adventure is an inconvenience rightly considered. - GK Chesterton

An actor's a guy, who if you ain't talking about him, ain't listening. - Marlon Brando

Absolute truth is a very rare and dangerous commodity in the context of professional journalism. - Hunter S. Thompson

War is fear cloaked in courage. - William Westmoreland

To be awake is to be alive. - Henry Thoreau

Success usually comes to those who are too busy to be looking for it. - Henry Thoreau

―――――⁓――――

If everyone demanded peace instead of another television set, then there'd be peace. - John Lennon

―――――⁓――――

I went out to the country so I could examine the simple things in life. - Henry Thoreau

―――――⁓――――

Honesty may be the best policy, but it's important to remember that apparently, by elimination, dishonesty is the second-best policy. - George Carlin

―――――⁓――――

Man is the only animal that blushes - or needs to. - Mark Twain

The best thing about the future is that it comes only one day at a time. - Abraham Lincoln

Anyone who invokes authors in discussion is not using his intelligence but his memory. - Leonardo da Vinci

Be not afraid of greatness. Some are born great, some achieve greatness, and some have greatness thrust upon 'em. - William Shakespeare

Please, if you ever see me getting beaten up by the police, please put your video camera down and help me. - Bobcat Goldthwait

For a small reward a man will hurry away on a long journey, while for eternal life many will hardly take a single step.

There is only one true friend who is always with you, in you and around you. He is god.

Profit in business comes from repeat customers, customers that boast about your project or service, and that bring friends with them. - W. Edwards Deming

---

Prayer is not asking, it is a longing of the soul.

Hide not your talents. They for use were made. What's a sundial in the shade? - Benjamin Franklin

---

Whenever someone asks me to define love, I usually think for a minute, then I spin around and pin the guy's arm behind his back. NOW who's asking the questions? - Jack Handey

The price of freedom is eternal vigilance. - Thomas Jefferson

Keep your eyes wide open before marriage, half shut afterwards. - Benjamin Franklin

An economist's guess is liable to be as good as anybody else's. - Will Rogers

Misfortune shows those who are not really friends. - Aristotle

High achievement always takes place in the framework of high expectation. - Charles Kettering

Friendship is unnecessary, like philosophy, like art. It has no survival value. Rather it is one of those things that give value to survival. - C. S. Lewis

If you're in a boxing match, try not to let the other guy's glove touch your lips, because you don't know where that glove has been. - Jack Handey

Can you imagine a world without men? No crime and lots of happy fat women. - Nicole Hollander

PRESIDENCY, n. The greased pig in the field game of American politics. - Ambrose Bierce

You can turn painful situations around through laughter. If you can find humor in anything, even poverty, you can survive it. - Bill Cosby

Set your goals high, and don't stop till you get there. - Bo Jackson

Anger is never without an argument, but seldom with a good one. - George Savile

I broke a mirror the other day. I'm supposed to get seven years of bad luck, but my lawyer thinks he can get me five. - Steven Wright

Refuse to be disturbed by anything. Refuse to be resentful or unhappy. And you will always be on top of the world.

You do not lead by hitting people over the head? That's assault, not leadership. - Dwight Eisenhower

In the Orthodox spiritual tradition, the ultimate moral question we ask is the following: Is what we are doing, is what I am doing, beautiful or not? - Carolyn Gifford

---

Until you've lost your reputation, you never realize what a burden it was or what freedom really is. - Margaret Mitchell

---

Poetry is what gets lost in translation. - Robert Frost

People who say they sleep like a baby usually don't have one. - Leo Burke

---

There are two kinds of failures: those who thought and never did, and those who did and never thought. - Laurence Peter

Keep away from people who try to belittle your ambitions. Small people always do that, but the really great make you feel that you, too, can become great. - Mark Twain

A bad thing is dear at any price.

Any new system is worth trying when your luck is bad. - Heywood Broun

Genuine poetry can communicate before it is understood. - T.S. Eliot

We who engage in nonviolent direct action are not the creators of tension. We merely bring to the surface the hidden tension that is already alive. - Martin Luther King Jr.

An election is coming. Universal peace is declared and the foxes have a sincere interest in prolonging the lives of the poultry. - T.S. Eliot

My political ideal is democracy. Everyone should be respected as individual, but no one idolized - Albert Einstein

Anyone who has lost track of time when using a computer knows the propensity to dream, the urge to make dreams come true and the tendency to miss lunch. - Tim Berners-Lee

I met in the street a very poor young man who was in love. His hat was old, his coat worn; his cloak was out at the elbows, the water passed through his shoes -- and the stars through his soul. - Victor Hugo

Guns aren't lawful; nooses give; gas smells awful. So you might as well live. - Dorothy Parker

The bird wishes it were a cloud, the cloud wishes it were a bird - Rabindranath Tagore

She was what we used to call a suicide blond - dyed by her own hand. - Saul Bellow

My idea of an agreeable person is a person who agrees with me. - Benjamin Disraeli

Everything is created twice first mentally and then physically - Greg Anderson

One can acquire everything in solitude except character. - Stendhal

---

Happiness serves hardly any other purpose than to make unhappiness possible. - Marcel Proust

---

When we're unemployed, we're called lazy; when the whites are unemployed it's called a depression. - Jesse Jackson

---

Unless Christianity is wholly false, the perception of ourselves which we have in moments of shame must be the only true one. - C.S. Lewis

---

We must govern from the middle, or we will not be able to govern at all – Senator Tom Daschle

Reform must come from within, not from without. You cannot legislate for virtue - Gibbobs

―――――〰―――――

People who live the most fulfilling lives are the ones who are always rejoicing at what they have.

―――――〰―――――

Movies can and do have tremendous influence in shaping young lives in the realm of entertainment towards the ideals and objectives of normal adulthood. - Walt Disney

―――――〰―――――

Neither man nor nation can exist without a sublime idea. - Fyodor Dostoevsky

―――――〰―――――

Never pick a fight with people who buy ink by the barrel. - Bill Clinton

Act quickly, think slowly

When good men die their goodness does not perish, but lives though they are gone. As for the bad, all that was theirs dies and is buried with them. - Euripides

History is more or less bunk. - Henry Ford

Your mind will give back exactly what you put into it.

Consciousness is either inexplicable illusion, or else revelation. - C.S. Lewis

It is most unwise for people in love to marry. - George Bernard Shaw

The surest way of spoiling a pleasure is to start examining your satisfaction. - C.S. Lewis

I don't know why I did it, I don't know why I enjoyed it, and I don't know why I'll do it again. - Socrates

Dying is a very dull, dreary affair. And my advice to you is to have nothing whatever to do with it. - W. Somerset Maugham

Four-fifths of all our troubles would disappear, if we would only sit down and keep still. - Calvin Coolidge

When the solution is simple, God is answering. -
Albert Einstein

In America, anyone can become president. That's one
of the risks you take. - Adlai Stevenson

There are two kinds of people, those who do the
work and those who take the credit. Try to be in the
first group; there is less competition there. - Indira
Gandhi

Actions will remove the doubt that theory cannot
solve.

A radical is a man with both feet firmly planted in
the air. - Franklin D. Roosevelt

Boredom is a vital problem for the moralist, since at least half the sins of mankind are caused by the fear of it. - Bertrand Russell

No one knows whether death, which people fear to be the greatest evil, may not be the greatest good. - Plato

If you are going to achieve excellence in big things, you develop the habit in little matters. Excellence is not an exception, it is a prevailing attitude. - Colin Powell

I do not know anyone who has got to the top without hard work. That is the recipe. It will not always get you to the top, but should get you pretty near. - Margaret Thatcher

Among people generally corrupt liberty cannot long exist. - Edmund Burke

Bitterness is like cancer. It eats upon the host. But anger is like fire. It burns it all clean. - Maya Angelou

A riot is the language of the unheard. - Martin Luther King Jr.

Nothing will ever be attempted if all possible objections must first be overcome. - Samuel Johnson

My experience is that as soon as people are old enough to know better, they don't know anything at all. - Oscar Wilde

He who can take no great interest in what is small will take false interest in what is great - John Ruskin

You can't depend on your eyes when your imagination is out of focus. - Mark Twain

Toleration is good for all, or it is good for none. - Edmund Burke

Make the love of God and the love of neighbor essentially present in your heart and soul.

Life is a fatal complaint, and an eminently contagious one. - Oliver Wendell Holmes

Some men would rather pursue happiness than obtain it. - Roger Ebert

I'm not upset about my divorce. I'm only upset I'm not a widow. - Roseanne Barr

Justice cannot be for one side alone, but must be for both. - Eleanor Roosevelt

A little inaccuracy sometimes saves tons of explanation. - H.H. Munro

Follow your dreams, for as you dream you shall become.

If there is a soul, it is a mistake to believe that it is given to us fully created. It is created here, throughout a whole life. And living is nothing else but that long and painful bringing forth. - Albert Camus

Government, even in its best state, is but a necessary evil; in its worst state, an intolerable one. - Thomas Paine

There are no strangers here; only friends you haven't yet met. - William Butler Yeats

The best thinking has been done in solitude. The worst has been done in turmoil. - Thomas Edison

Word of mouth is the best and more cost effective form of marketing - Allen Schneeberger

It is easier to prevent bad habits than to break them. - Benjamin Franklin

People often say that motivation doesn't last. Well, neither does bathing that's why we recommend it daily. - Zig Ziglar

I sacrifice to no god save myself? And to my belly, greatest of deities. - Euripides

I do not consider it an insult, but rather a compliment to be called an agnostic. I do not pretend to know where many ignorant men are sure -- that is all that agnosticism means. - Clarence Darrow

Four are the things I'd have been better without: love, curiosity, freckles and doubt. - Dorothy Parker

Nothing inspires forgiveness quite like revenge. - Scott Adams

We live in an age when unnecessary things are our only necessities. - Oscar Wilde

Freedom is not America's gift to the world; it is the Almighty God's gift to every man and woman in this world. - George W. Bush

Great truths can only be forgotten and can never be falsified. - GK Chesterton

Life in abundance comes only through great love. - Elbert Hubbard

The only way to have a friend is to be one. - Ralph Waldo Emerson

---

The advice of their elders to young men is very apt to be as unreal as a list of the hundred best books. - Oliver Wendell Holmes

---

Most writers regard truth as their most valuable possession, and therefore are most economical in its use. - Mark Twain

---

Not only is there no God, but try finding a plumber on Sunday. - Woody Allen

---

Too many of us are not living our dreams because we are living our fears - Les Brown

You must either modify your dreams or magnify your skills. - Jim Rohn

Individual commitment to a group effort -- that is what makes a team work a company work, a society work, a civilization work. - Vince Lombardi

The Social Contract is nothing more or less than a vast conspiracy of human beings to lie to and humbug themselves and one another for the general good. Lies are the mortar that binds the savage individual man into the social masonry. - H.G. Wells

No one can make you feel inferior without your consent. - Eleanor Roosevelt

Providence protects children and idiots. I know because I have tested it. - Mark Twain

***

He who sows courtesy reaps friendship, and he who plants kindness gathers love.

***

Christmas is a time when everybody wants his past forgotten and his present remembered. - Phyllis Diller

***

Moral indignation is jealousy with a halo. - H.G. Wells

***

When you work seven days a week, fourteen hours a day, you get lucky. - Armand Hammer

***

Life's greatest achievement is the continuous remaking of yourself so that at last you know how to live.

When you break the big laws, you do not get freedom; you do not even get anarchy. You get the small laws. - GK Chesterton

Life isn't worth living unless you are willing to take some big chances.

More than half modern culture depends on what one shouldn't read. - Oscar Wilde

It was impossible to get a conversation going, everybody was talking too much. - Yogi Berra

My advice to you is to get married. If you find a good wife you'll be happy; if not you'll become a philosopher. - Socrates

---

Art is a kind of innate drive that seizes a human being and makes him its instrument. The artist is not a person endowed with free will who seeks his own ends, but one who allows art to realize its purpose through him. - Carl Jung

---

Courage is being scared to death, but saddling up anyway. - John Wayne

---

The MPAA rates this PG-13. It is too vulgar for anyone under 13, and too dumb for anyone over 13. - Roger Ebert

---

Fanaticism consists of redoubling your efforts when you have forgotten your aim. - George Santayana

---

The Americans combine the notions of Christianity and of liberty so intimately in their minds, that it is impossible to make them conceive the one without the other. - Alexis de Tocqueville

---

I've had a wonderful time, but this wasn't it. - Groucho Marx

---

The books we read should be chosen with great care, that they may be, as an Egyptian king wrote over his library, "The medicines of the soul." - Oliver Wendell Holmes

---

My second favorite household chore is ironing. My first being hitting my head on the top bunk bed until I faint. - Erna Bombeck

I do not believe one can settle how much we ought to give. I am afraid the only safe rule is to give more than we can spare. - C.S. Lewis

Courage is like love; it must have hope for nourishment. - Napoleon Bonaparte

There are those who hate Christianity and call their hatred an all-embracing love for all religions. - GK Chesterton

Our hearts grow tender with childhood memories and love of kindred, and we are better throughout the year for having, in spirit, become a child again at Christmas time. - Laura Ingalls Wilder

Fiction is the truth inside the lie. - Stephen King

The best way to win an argument is to begin by being right. - Jill Ruckleshaus

Experience is that marvelous thing that enables you to recognize a mistake when you make it again. - Franklin Jones

We don't know a millionth of one percent about anything. - Thomas Edison

There is only one religion, the religion of love. There is only one language, the language of heart.

In the theater, you go from point A to point Z, building your performance as the evening progresses. You have to relinquish that control on a film. - Gwyneth Paltrow

---

Better than a thousand hollow words, is one word that brings peace. - Siddhartha Buddha

---

I made a wrong mistake. - Yogi Berra

He is a very modest man with a great deal to be modest about. - Winston Churchill

---

The greatest mistake you can make in life is to be continually fearing you will make one. - Elbert Hubbard

Perhaps one of the most important accomplishments of my administration has been minding my own business. - Calvin Coolidge

Humor is perhaps a sense of intellectual perspective: an awareness that some things are really important, others not; and that the two kinds are most oddly jumbled in everyday affairs. - Christopher Morely

Genius is only the power of making continuous efforts. - Elbert Hubbard

When we got into office, the thing that surprised me the most was that things were as bad as we'd been saying they were. - John F. Kennedy

Circumstances are the rulers of the weak; they are but the instruments of the wise.

The variety of all things forms a pleasure. - Euripides

I continue to find my greatest pleasure, and so my reward, in the work that precedes what the world calls success. - Thomas Edison

It is better to be violent, if there is violence in our hearts, than to put on the cloak of nonviolence to cover impotence. - Mahatma Gandhi

Trust the man who hesitates in his speech and is quick and steady in action, but beware of long arguments and long beards. - George Santayana

In this country we have no place for hyphenated Americans. - Theodore Roosevelt

They defend their errors as if they were defending their inheritance. - Edmund Burke

The best and noblest lives are those which are set towards high ideals.

Better keep yourself clean and bright; you are the window through which you must see the world. - George Bernard Shaw

Life is just one grand sweet song, so start the music. - Ronald Reagan

---

I figure wherever I am, that's the place to be. - Tommy Lasorda

---

My toughest fight was with my first wife. - Muhammad Ali

A superior man is modest in his speech, but exceeds in his actions. - Confucius

---

Being religious means asking passionately the question of the meaning of our existence and being willing to receive answers, even if the answers hurt. - Paul Tillich

The average Hollywood film stars ambition is to be admired by an American, courted by an Italian, married to an Englishman, and have a French boyfriend. - Katharine Hepburn

---

Some of our principal regrets in life are the opportunities we missed and the chances we didn't take.

If liberty and equality, as is thought by some, are chiefly to be found in democracy, they will be best attained when all persons alike share in government to the utmost. - Aristotle

---

Over grown military establishments are under any form of government inauspicious to liberty, and are to be regarded as particularly hostile to republican liberty. - George Washington

---

A man who is eating or lying with his wife or preparing to go to sleep in humility, thankfulness and temperance, is, by Christian standards, in an infinitely higher state than one who is listening to Bach or reading Plato in a state of pride. - C.S. Lewis

We humans do not need to leave Earth to get to a hostile, deadly, alien environment; we already have Miami. - Dave Barry

Beauty is ever to the lonely mind a shadow fleeting; she is never plain. She is a visitor who leaves behind the gift of grief, the souvenir of pain. - Christopher Morley

The soul of man is immortal and imperishable. - Plato

The force of public opinion cannot be resisted when permitted freely to be expressed. The agitation it produces must be submitted to. - Thomas Jefferson

Photography is more than a medium for factual communication of ideas. It is a creative art. - Ansel Adams

We have just enough religion to make us hate, but not enough to make us love one another. - Jonathan Swift

Put your hand on a hot stove for a minute, and it seems like an hour. Sit with a pretty girl for an hour, and it seems like a minute. THAT'S relativity. - Albert Einstein

ABOUT THE AUTHOR

Growing up in a small town in India, Susheel heard a story. A child goes to a fair and sees a man selling balloons; he watches the red balloon fly away high into the sky. He asks the balloon vendor, "Will the green balloon fly into the sky as well?" The balloon man says, "Yes." Next the child asks, "How about the black balloon?" The balloon vendor replies, "It is not the color of the balloon, but what is in it that takes the balloon high into the sky."

Susheel has lived with a strong belief that "it is what you have in you, that takes you the places you want to go, it does not matter where you come from, all that matters is where you are going."

Susheel has a passion for quotes, sayings, and studying interesting facts about history and their relevance in the modern world. In the past decade, he has consulted with fortune 500 clients advising them on business strategies.